PRAISE FOR
EMBRACING THE MONSTER

"In a very poignant and honest way, Veronica Crawford shares her life journey as an individual with learning and attentional problems. She courageously describes the pain and humiliation she experienced growing up, the self-defeating coping strategies she initially used to deal with her distress, and her eventual path toward self-acceptance and accomplishment. The information Veronica provides, together with the invaluable insights of Dr. Larry B. Silver, will validate what many individuals with hidden disabilities experience and will help others to understand the struggles of these individuals. Veronica's success and resilience will serve as an inspiration for all who read this wonderful book. Her journey is a testimony to the power of hope and the human spirit."

Robert Brooks, Ph.D.
Faculty
Harvard Medical School
Author, *The Self-Esteem Teacher*,
and co-author, *Raising Resilient Children*

"An inspiring work, laying bare the heart, mind, and soul of a truly resilient individual. This book should be required reading for parents, professionals, educators, and all those struggling to understand and overcome a hidden disability."

Sam Goldstein, Ph.D.
Clinical neuropsychologist and school psychologist
University of Utah
Co-author, *Raising Resilient Children*
and *Learning Disabilities and Challenging Behaviors:
A Guide to Intervention and Classroom Management*

"In this intimate, personal narrative, Veronica Crawford captures the psychological, social, and scholastic challenges associated with growing up and living with learning disabilities. Her revealing tale will help professionals develop empathy and understanding of the academic, as well as the emotional aspects of coping with these difficulties. Her story speaks clearly to individuals who have hidden disabilities and will promote self-understanding, acceptance, hope, optimism, and resilience—the necessary ingredients for shaping a successful future."

Nancy Mather, Ph.D.
Associate Professor
University of Arizona, Tucson
Co-author, *Learning Disabilities and Challenging Behaviors:*
A Guide to Intervention and Classroom Management

"Veronica shares her poignant story of life with long-undiagnosed and, hence, untreated, learning disabilities and attention-deficit/ hyperactivity disorder. She sensitizes us to the pervasiveness of these problems and reminds us that their impact is felt far beyond the classroom, in every aspect of daily life. It is a painful but hopeful story, suggesting that self-understanding is the first step on the road to self-acceptance and self-love for individuals with learning problems."

Arlyn Roffman, Ph.D.
Professor of Special Education
Lesley College, Cambridge, Massachusetts
Author, *Meeting the Challenges of Learning Disabilities in Adulthood*

Embracing the Monster

Embracing the Monster

OVERCOMING THE CHALLENGES OF HIDDEN DISABILITIES

by

Veronica Crawford

with commentary by

Larry B. Silver, M.D.

·PAUL·H·
BROOKES
PUBLISHING CO

Baltimore • London •Toronto • Sydney

Paul H. Brookes Publishing Co.
Post Office Box 10624
Baltimore, Maryland 21285-0624

www.brookespublishing.com

Typeset by Integrated Publishing Solutions, Grand Rapids, Michigan.
Manufactured in the United States of America by Versa Press,
East Peoria, Illinois.

The situations described in this book are based on the author's actual experiences. Many of the names have been changed and identifying details have been altered to protect confidentiality. Though none of it has been created *ex nihilo*, much of the dialogue here has been re-created from memory, with whatever fallibility that implies.

JUST WAIT
Music and words by John Popper
Copyright © 1994 by Blues Traveler Publishing Co.
All Rights Reserved.
Reprinted by Permission.

THE END OF THE WORLD
Music by Arthur Kent
Words by Sylvia Dee
Copyright © 1962 (Renewed) by Music Sales
Corporation (ASCAP) and Edward Proffitt Music
International Copyright Secured. All Rights Reserved.
Reprinted by Permission.

Library of Congress Cataloging-in-Publication Data

Crawford, Veronica.
    Embracing the monster : overcoming the challenges of hidden
disabilities / by Veronica Crawford ; with commentary by Larry B. Silver.
        p.   cm.
    Includes bibliographical references.
    ISBN 1-55766-522-2
    1. Crawford, Veronica.   2. Learning disabled—United States—Biography.
    3. Learning disabilities.   I. Silver, Larry B.   II. Title.
LC4818.5 .C73 2001
371.94—dc21
[B]   2001037583
                                                                        CIP

British Library Cataloguing in Publication data are available from the
British Library.

To my husband Rob, who has shown me
how to accept who I am, to love myself,
and to know that I only have to be myself to be loved

To my kids for what they have taught me:

my son Justin, who has shown me
so much of myself
through his struggles and triumphs,
and my daughter Tess, who has allowed me
to believe in the beauty
each person has to offer this world

To Erika, Devin, and Ciera, my stepchildren

To my parents, who had the courage
to challenge me, to push me,
and to learn more about me as I became an adult;
they gave me courage to continue reaching for my goals

A special dedication to the memory of my young-adult friend Jon,
who struggled in his world of confusion.
His life ended tragically—he committed suicide—
which served to remind me why we must keep trying to find answers and help
for people with hidden disabilities

And to all of you, my extended family members,
professionals, and individuals with whom I have worked.
You know who you are! I love you all!

CONTENTS

Contents

ABOUT THE AUTHORS

Veronica Crawford, M.A., Program Director, Life Development Institute, 18001 North 79th Avenue, Suite E, Glendale, AZ 85308

Veronica Crawford has vast experience working with individuals with learning, attention, and co-morbid diagnoses. She is a senior disabilities analyst certified by the American Board of Medical Psychotherapists and Psychodiagnosticians, who, in addition to serving as Program Director for the Life Development Institute, owns a small company that writes transition and life care plans for individuals with disabilities. Veronica's unique experiences—both personal and professional—add to her ability to mentor, advise, and counsel many with hidden disabilities. For those who know, work with, or care about someone with hidden disabilities, Veronica's insights and expertise offer a much clearer understanding of an individual's daily challenges. She offers a variety of positive ways to help individuals, families, and professionals find success and a better quality of life for themselves and others who care about them.

Veronica has presented more than 300 programs nationwide to families, educators, employers, and professionals on the experiences she has had as a resilient individual with multiple hidden disabilities. She has co-written a chapter for the book, *Clinical Interventions for Adult ADHD: A Comprehensive Approach (Academic Press, 2002)*. *Embracing the Monster: Overcoming the Challenges of Hidden Disabilities* is her first book.

WITH CONTRIBUTIONS FROM

Larry B. Silver, M.D., Montrose Professional Park, 6286 Montrose Road, Rockville, Maryland 20852

Dr. Larry B. Silver is a child and adolescent psychiatrist in private practice in the Washington, D.C., area. He is also Clinical Professor of Psychiatry at the Georgetown University School of Medicine. Prior to holding these positions, Dr. Silver was Acting Director and Deputy Director of the National Institute of Mental Health (NIMH) in Bethesda, Maryland. Dr. Silver has also served as Professor of Psychiatry, Professor of Pediatrics, and Chief of Child and Adolescent Psychiatry at the Robert Wood Johnson School of Medicine.

Dr. Silver is a well-known author in the areas of learning disabilities and attention-deficit/hyperactivity disorder (ADHD) as well as of other common mental health issues for children and adolescents. Dr. Silver has been very active in service to the profession and has been a strong advocate for individuals with learning disabilities. He was serving as President of the Learning Disabilities Association of America in 2001.

FOREWORD

Life is challenging for most people. To have any disability is an even greater challenge in life. To have a hidden disability is an added challenge. Others cannot see or understand it. Thus, they can only conclude that the individual is doing things on purpose: He or she is lazy, unmotivated, or bad. Individuals with hidden disabilities may be equally unaware of the problems. They often don't even realize that their brains function in ways different from those of others. Soon, they begin to believe what they are told: They must be lazy or unmotivated. Perhaps they are just not trying hard enough. "Maybe I'm just not very bright," they think to themselves.

Until Veronica's early adult years, when she received a formal diagnosis, her hidden problems—her learning disabilities and her attention-deficit/hyperactivity disorder—were seen by her family, teachers, friends, and others as evidence that she was unmotivated and that she was not trying. Some people who knew her believed that she was lazy or lacking intelligence. Those who knew her were confused by the paradoxes they saw. She often fell behind in her studies, yet she was uniquely gifted in some nonacademic areas. She was charming and social, yet she suffered from inner shyness and experienced difficulty in making "real" friends. She accepted the only explanation she could for her chronic failures: She must be bad and stupid.

As a professional reading Veronica's book, it is difficult for me to understand how teachers, year after year, did not see her learning disabilities, language disabilities, sensory integration dysfunction, and her emotional problems. These struggles were all too apparent. What a different life she might have had if these difficulties had been recognized and addressed in childhood.

At the same time, I am not surprised that Veronica's struggles went undiagnosed so long. Every day I see children and adolescents in my practice who have similar hidden challenges that have not been identified. They come to me because they have behavioral or social problems or are "unmotivated" in school. And, like Veronica, just under the surface they feel pain, sadness, and frustration. These children and adolescents come into my office expecting me to be another adult who is frustrated or angry at their lack of success in school. Instead, I might start by saying, "School seems so difficult for you. I know you want to do well. Help me understand your problems so that I can find a way to help you." For some, this is the first time they have ever described their difficulties with school. This makes me question the motivations of those who have failed to seek the source of these individuals' pain and difficulties: Why do people still yell at the smoke rather than try to find the fire?

Veronica had to survive. She coped by covering up, faking, and seeking friends' help. Sometimes these methods worked, and sometimes they did not. As an academically and emotionally wounded adolescent and young adult, she survived by using fewer constructive and increasingly self-destructive ways. Yet, it is not difficult to understand the road she traveled. We all have to survive, and at a price.

As we read the chapter that ends the narrative portion of the book (Chapter 8), we learn that she did survive. This is the message of hope she gives. It was not until after high school that her hidden problems were recognized and addressed. As those hidden disabilities became apparent to all, including to herself, she was able to get the help that should have been there when she was a child. Her emotional difficulties were identified and treated. Her lifetime of pain was not as easy to overcome, however. Her self-esteem and self-image are markedly improved. Yet, under the surface, problems remain and resurface from time to time.

I met Veronica when she was a young adult. I know her now as a friend and a colleague. She is a bright, competent young woman who is a successful person, wife, mother, and professional. But, when I am with her, I sometimes sense the insecurity and pain that can surface all so quickly when she has to struggle or when something reminds her of the past. Still, she pauses, understands, accepts, and goes on. This is the inner strength that helped her to survive and that continues to help her face each day.

Veronica's willingness to reveal her life story is both brave and risky. Disclosing is always risky. She is willing to take this risk in the hope that she will help others. I admire her courage in doing this. Veronica, in her wish to help others, reveals much about herself. She shares her innermost feelings and thoughts as she was growing up. Parents and teachers need to understand Veronica: her childhood, her adolescence, her young adulthood, and her adult years. They must understand her feelings and her thoughts, her sadness and her pain. She shares a window on what it is like to have hidden disabilities. This awareness may help others to recognize a "Veronica" in their lives. Some readers with hidden disabilities will see *themselves* on the pages of this book. Veronica hopes that by understanding her, these people will gain the strength to understand themselves. She hopes that they will feel safe in revealing themselves to others who might be able to help.

Veronica's pleas throughout this story are to those who are so important to children, adolescents, and adults with hidden disabilities. Her message is clear: Don't just point out the problems. Don't take the easy way out and blame the person with the problems. Don't criticize and assume that the person is acting or performing the way he or she is because that individual chooses to do so. See the struggles. See the pain. See that the person does not want to fail or to appear inappropriate. Look for the reasons for the problems. If someone cannot read or write, don't get angry that they cannot read or write. Try to find out the reason behind the problem so that he or she can be helped. Only then can the hidden disabilities be brought to light. And, with recognition, help can be provided.

Veronica's message to all people with hidden problems is a hopeful one. The past cannot be changed. Understand it. Use this understanding to explain the present and to help in changing the future. Veronica, thank you not only for taking the risk of revealing your disabilities and how you have to constantly strive not to let them defeat you but also for revealing your most personal pain and struggles. Your courage will give hope and courage to others.

Larry B. Silver, M.D.

ACKNOWLEDGMENTS

There have been so many people that have touched my life in many ways—my parents, sister, children, counselors, teachers, friends, and even former loves. But the most significant people who have helped me in the years that were perhaps the most difficult, my adult years, are two men who helped me realize that I had much to offer and they had nothing to gain. Their efforts are and continue to be selfless, their love unconditional. They are the reason I moved forward with the very difficult task of rewriting more than 14 drafts to finally reach the book that you now hold in your hands.

Dr. Larry Silver is not one to desire any form of attention; his acts of love toward other humans are not driven by the need for recognition but are based on knowing what it feels like to be appreciated, believed in, supported, and loved. Dr. Larry Silver touched my life at a time I was ready to give up. In 1994, I felt I had lost my entire world, my meaning, my purpose. He felt my sadness from across a lunch table, tossed an orange at me (fortunately I caught it), and asked me to take a short walk with him. During this walk, I was shocked by the accuracy of his insights and by his invitation to stay in touch as I found my way out of the darkness. He told me I had a lot to offer others like myself and that I deserved to be happy. He encouraged me to move forward with my dream to start my own business and to continue to speak. He shook my hand, smiled at me, and said he enjoyed our walk and then said goodbye, never asking for a thing in return. This man was not like any others I had met (except my own father) but a famous person in the LD field who thought I had something to offer the world. It was that moment when I began to see some light in the clouds of my mind.

Larry and I stayed in touch for many years. Once in a while I'd write or call. When I told him I was writing this book, he asked to read it, explaining that he reviewed many books and could only endorse those that he felt were a positive and accurate depiction of the issues facing those with LD. After he read the draft he called and told me that it made him cry, it made him laugh, and it gave him hope. He offered to do more than endorse my book: He offered to write the foreword and help me find a publisher! I continued to stay in touch with Larry and would see him at conferences from time to time. We had this emerging family bond; I consider Larry to be a second father to me, although I never really told him this for many years.

My husband Rob, like Larry, is generous and kind. When I met him, Rob struck me as someone who really knew a lot about the field of LD, had a good business mind, and had tremendous compassion. For years I would see Rob occasionally at conferences and eventually, I was invited to be a part of his circle of friends. He saw in me potential that I did not know I had: that I was an untapped spokesperson and a woman who could provide a positive voice for others with learning disabilities. Rob was my friend first, then eventually my husband—for me, this was a perfect way for a relationship to bloom. I needed to know I was cared for, respected, and loved as a person; this he was able to offer. Rob has truly taught me how to be a friend. He has seen me through many dark moments. We have spent many endless evenings talking all night when I have been manic. He was always there, never waning in his love, understanding, or compassion. He would listen, offer loving advice and support, and hold me when he knew I needed to be held.

When I tackled rewrites of this book, Rob was an inspiration, providing encouragement, suggestions, and unwavering belief in me. There were times as I drafted this book over and over that I would cry, scream, threaten to burn it, and declare that it was trash. I just couldn't get it right, something was wrong with it; then, out of the blue, Rob read draft #11 and said that its strength was in the way in which I tell my life's journey. He advised me to remove the didactic wording and turn it into a true story. After three additional rounds of revisions with Paul H. Brookes Publishing Co., the book was complete!

I love Rob and Larry; I respect them, admire them, and consider them to be angels in my life. I have never met two other people who will sit with me when I am down, tolerate me when I am up, listen to my concerns and fears, never pass judgment, and never ever walk away. It is solely the two of them who have held me up long enough for me to learn that I have a reason to go on; for this I thank them both for all they have given me, their unconditional love.

And, although both Rob and Larry were instrumental in bringing this book to life, several others believed in this project as well: Dr. Sam Goldstein, Dr. Robert Brooks, Dr. Arlyn Roffman and Dr. Nancy Mather. Their encouragement helped me immensely. These experts in the field—truly charismatic adults in my life—kept me going, telling me I had that ability.

INTRODUCTION

GAZING INTO THE LOOKING GLASS

"But, you're so attractive!" To many people these are words that invoke a smile, or perhaps a little embarrassment, but to me, these words are a warning: The gun is about to go off, and I am in the line of fire.

I can't count the times throughout my life when I have been complimented about the way I look. Unfortunately, the compliments usually precede some more negative observation or opinion. It doesn't matter who is giving the compliment; it matters how it is said. When it is spoken with the word "but" in front of it, I know it is a sign of disbelief.

What the person is really saying is something such as "You can't be learning disabled, you're too attractive" or "She's lying, how could she have a learning disability?" Or, as a college professor told me once (very quietly so no one else would hear), "You know, you're such an attractive young woman, you shouldn't let anyone know you're LD." I remember laughing at that statement. I had just recently gotten the courage to disclose my disabilities. Little did I know that such disclosure would be a double-edged sword for years to come.

This book was a struggle for me. I began writing it in 1990, put it down, picked it up, and did not know what to do with it. Now, more than a decade later, after many tears, much work, many rejections, and many changes, I have accomplished the goal of a lifetime. The process of writing this book was an experience in both pain and self-acceptance. It became evident to those who helped me edit this book (including a wonderful editor at Paul H. Brookes Publishing Co.) that I did indeed have significant learning disabilities. Sometimes when you know someone, when you have always seen the end results, the rough drafts are then so shocking, the reactions so disbelieving. And it is these types of reactions that encouraged me to press on with the book.

It is my intent to share with you some of the most private aspects of my life: the events, the feelings, and the emotionality of dealing with being "different." I have met and worked with many people who also have LD as well as other hidden disabilities. People have shared so many similar stories with me and frequently express having been embarrassed in trying to talk to others openly for fear of rejection. I have seen that rejection; I have experienced that pain. I know what it is like to have both extreme strengths and extreme weaknesses, and having them so intertwined that getting the strengths to shine because of the weaknesses is impossible without help and accommodations.

I wrote this book not for me, but for you. I wrote it for the professionals (e.g., teachers, counselors, psychologists and psychiatrists, social workers) who want to and/or need to understand and find a way to help people who live with hidden disabilities. I wrote it for the parent who agonizes with what will happen to his or her child, who sees the child's struggles and wonders how to help and if things will get better. But mostly, I wrote it for those of you, like me, who feel you are alone. I hope that in this book you will find you are *not* alone, that despite your internal anguish you will find hope.

If we are going to help others understand hidden disabilities and how growing up with hidden disabilities affects a person's whole life, we have to be honest. I know that sharing the significance of my having learning disabilities (LD), attention-deficit/hyperactivity disorder (ADHD), and bipolar disorder, along with the losses I have endured in my life due to the psychological impact of these disabilities, places me at risk of more emotional harm. The reward is greater than the risk, however. This book may be a gift—a reason to go on for those who struggle behind a shield that covers their own competence.

It is time to clear this path, to understand that LD or ADHD or other hidden disabilities are *real* disabilities that affect life daily. They not only affect the academic realm, but emotional, personal/ social, educational, and career aspects as well. As is true of most things in life, having a learning disability or any hidden disability has it ups and downs. But the downs are more frequent and are not all due to the disability. Some are caused by how society has traditionally perceived them. It is the combination of the disability and the responses to the disability that creates personal disruption and devastation.

To truly empathize, we need first to understand the people involved, how they feel, and their great need for acceptance of self and a feeling of acceptance from others. Once our understanding grows, then we can improve their chances for success. These individuals have the types of disabilities that create doubt in people's minds because they cannot be seen. These are the disabilities that cause those who have them to doubt themselves, often leaving them without a purpose, a goal, and a dream. We must allow them to see. We must not let ignorance be the cause of human destruction.

I often wonder what tomorrow will bring. Will I have a good day, or will I get frustrated and need to get past the anger, the hurt, the reminder that I have to keep proving myself over and over (to me and to others)? What will trigger the anger? Will I be trying to read a map while lost in a strange city, or will I be trying to remember how to use a bank machine while people are standing in line behind me expressing their frustration? Will it be the fact that I cannot recognize an arrow direction, causing me to turn the wrong way down a hall or to become lost? Will it be at a checkout counter when the clerk loudly points out the correct spelling of the store's name? Who knows! One thing is for sure—not a day goes by that I am not confronted with something that is a direct link to my learning disabilities, attention problem, or mood disorders. That is a fact. But the key is in how I will cope with the problem. The answer is how I learned to cope with it, and how I—like a person who is blind—learned to find a way around the barrier.

When I write this, sometimes I feel that I am having an out-of-body experience: This can't be me; how could I have earned a master's degree, held a management position with a Fortune 100 company, and started my own business? One would have thought that, by now, I would be past having to prove myself to anyone, including myself. But I guess, as it is said in a song by Blues Traveler, "Your uphill struggles leave you headed downhill." Of course they do; life always has ups and downs—it's all in how you look at those things. Some people believe I have a hidden agenda and that I am lying about having these hidden disabilities. How could I really have an IQ score that is borderline average and accomplish so much? How could I have such poor reading, math, and language skills yet create, articulate, and problem solve at advanced levels? Some people believe that I have gotten where I am because I am attractive or because I am manipulative. It's true, I have been manipulative, but the price paid was my own, including my loss of self-esteem, my depression, and my suicide ideation. My personal losses were extreme.

It's true that I have been successful; it's true that the reason for my success was because I was resilient; but how was it that I was so able to succeed with all the negative experiences I have encountered? It's because I was shown that what I lack in some areas I make up for in others, and I refuse to give up and let anyone else win. I want to take this opportunity to remind people that we have to work together, not separately. We need to build supportive foundations for people with hidden disabilities; not barricades. The reality is that we *will* face these barricades, but the way in which we use tools to get around them is the question and the solution.

It is most important that we teach others by our own examples, that we understand these complex disabilities, and that we support the ups and downs and the apparent oddities that go along with these disabilities. We need to acknowledge that the real world is certainly difficult for everyone, not just for people with learning disabilities; but it is less easy to negotiate this difficult world when you have hidden disabilities.

Having LD is not just an academic problem, having ADHD is not just an attention problem, having sensory integration dysfunction is not just a problem with physical reaction, and having mental illness does not mean a person has to be out of work, institutionalized, or on the streets. The emotional effects of having these disorders are something that cannot be ignored, or we are just heaping problems on top of problems. We have to look at what the problems are, develop strategies, and help people to become independent, not dependent.

I believe the secret to success is intrinsic with supported pushes from extrinsic sources such as friends, family, and professional resources. Support can come from a person or people who leave lasting positive reminders, or create a voice, a clear voice, in the mind of a person struggling with seeing through the confusion. Read on and you will begin to understand that there is always hope to continue no matter what barriers, what traumas one endures. There is a way. It is important for you to know as well that I am not a genius; my measured intelligence is not anywhere near the gifted range, in fact it is in the low average range. You may read this and wonder how I sound so eloquent in this book. The ideas, emotions, and images are mine, but the book has been edited by the publisher to make it easier to read. The spelling and grammar mistakes, with which I still struggle, have been corrected for the most part. For example, here is a passage from Chapter 4 as I originally wrote it:

For some students, high school is a place one looks forward to going. For others, they could take it or leave it. And still, for others like me, they dreaded going, staying, or coming back the next day. Even after high school, dreams would haunt me, fearing having to return to high school over and over again. The dream consisted of not having graduated and having to do it all over again still haunts me today, even after earning masters degree.

This was edited to read as follows:

Some students look forward to high school. Others can take it or leave it. And still others, like me, dreaded going, staying after, or coming back the next day. Even after I graduated from high school, I would dream of not having graduated and of having to do it all over again—a thought that still haunts me today, even though I have earned a master's degree.

I disclose this to encourage you to see that each person has different abilities, different limitations; my disabilities affect me daily, but I have learned to rely on my strengths. I learned to be realistic in my choices; this was my method in finding success. My hope is that this book will help you find yours.

Embracing the Monster

1

HUMPTY DUMPTY, BROKEN INTO PIECES

BIRTH THROUGH THE PRESCHOOL YEARS

You step into this
funhouse and your whole
world is altered. You
become lost. For a while
it's fun, but imagine what
it would be like being
trapped in this funhouse
every day?

They say that little girls are different from little boys. They say that little girls are made of sugar and spice and everything nice; little boys are made of snakes and snails and puppy dogs' tails. I wonder what happened to the sugar and spice when they were handing it out to me? Oh, it's not that bad, actually. I was a beautiful baby (or so my parents have told me). I was born in Germany into a military family. It wasn't many years ago that my mother told me that a person isn't in the military alone; the whole family is enlisted. All the packing and moving—never being settled—is a lot to deal with. In hindsight, I am sure that if it hadn't been for this military lifestyle, we would have discovered my disabilities sooner. I wouldn't have been able to hide and run from these problems that I envisioned collectively as a "monster." Perhaps, as well, if we had lived in only one or two locations, my parents would have been able to see my struggles and difficulties more clearly and would have attributed them to something neurological rather than to the moves.

I was the youngest of three children: I had one sister and one brother, both of whom were as normal (whatever normal is) as two kids can get. I was born full term with no complications. Mother told me that I was born so fast the doctor barely made it to the hospital to "catch" me. Dad waited outside the delivery room, which was common back then. He was surprised to hear me rejoicing on my entry into the world so quickly. Little did he know that the sounds of my infant cry would turn into a constant internal cry of pain as I grew up in a world filled with confusion and overstimulation.

When I asked my parents to reflect on my babyhood, their first statement was that I was too good; I was so easy—I didn't really fuss about anything and didn't even cry often. I enjoyed eating, and I loved to be bounced, almost endlessly. In their eyes, I was just a beautiful baby. It wasn't until it was time for me to start communicating that they began to be concerned. Although my parents worried about my difficulty in communicating, learning disabilities, or other mild developmental delays, these were not recognized as a problem during that time period. Unless a child had severe developmental delays, nothing was done; after all, every child develops at a different time and in a different way.

The next part of my life, the toddler through preschool years, is difficult for me to write about because it was a time before I understood words and the meanings behind them. I knew a few words at age 2, but I really didn't talk until I was 3 years old. My vocabulary was inappropriate for a 3-year-old. I used the wrong words for things quite frequently. For example, when I asked for milk, I really wanted juice. I had a lot to say in my mind but the words weren't coming out right. I remember becoming frustrated when I tried to tell others what I wanted. Even then I knew something was different about me. Though I can't remember exact events, I can remember the feelings connected with the images in my mind. My mother and father, when reading this chapter, were

Veronica at age 6 months

amazed at my ability to remember things associated with specific events at such a young age.

We moved from Germany to Albuquerque, New Mexico, before I was 2 years old. I remember some things about New Mexico: the house, the yard, and the Burger Chef sign you could see over the concrete fence in our back yard. Mom, Dad, Grandma, my brother and sister, and our dog, Penny, all lived in a small, but very nice, clean, and orderly house. My parents told me years ago that at that time I was an affectionate child, almost to an extreme. I still enjoyed being held and hugging others. I was very trusting and open to others, and I was eager to please, even at that young age.

I was, however, a very curious child. Though words did not come easily to me, I did not lack mobility, and I was investigative to the point of personal harm. One time while my brother and I were horsing around, I was riding on his back and I fell off. My parents tell me that they didn't know until the next day that I had broken my collarbone. Their first concern was that I might have a concussion and they were told to watch me, but I didn't complain about the pain in my collarbone and my cries were no different than normal.

Another time I lit myself on fire! I have always been intrigued by fire; it somehow places me into a hypnotic state. Even today I can become hyper-focused in the flicker of light from a flame. I can recall small pieces of this event. My father was lighting a fire in the small fireplace. Dad is a meticulous man with a system for everything. He was always very careful, almost methodical about his activities. He always planned everything, step by step, until it became routine. That day was no different from the others; he lit the fire by rolling a newspaper into a long cylinder, lighting it with a match, and stuffing the cylinder into the fireplace, where more newspapers were piled neatly under the kindling and logs. There was no screen covering the opening, and as soon as he left, I repeated his actions. It was not unusual for me to try to repeat what my father did, no matter what the consequences. I am sure I had watched my father light the fire many times, studying and memorizing how he did it and perhaps waiting for the right moment to try it on my own. Perhaps in an impulsive moment, I made the move to duplicate his task. I succeeded, but instead of letting go, I held on to the paper and lit it to my hair. I forgot one important step in the process, however, to place the lit fire in the "stone cave." Fortunately for me, my mother appeared as the fire singed my hair, eyebrows, and the surface of the skin on my head. I was left uninjured with no visible scars and only a less-than-attractive head of hair.

Almost all kids have accidents and get into things, and it's not a big deal. But my incidents occurred one after another and involved very hazardous conditions. Also interesting in my case was that I did not seem to retain the learning from my mistakes. For example, I would follow my father up the ladder to the roof, repeatedly. Even after I had been told not to follow him up the ladder and been swatted to discourage me from doing it, I would just go on up that ladder anyway; to me, a ladder must be climbed!

We left New Mexico to move to California when I was 3 years old. My dad had been given orders to go to Vietnam. I am still haunted by the memory of the day we drove Dad to the airport. I was in the back of our yellow station wagon; it was a clear day. With most of my memories, I can play these types of images back almost like a movie. This is not unusual; many times children with the types of disabilities I have are very tuned in to little details, remembering colors, smells. (This hyperattentiveness often is mistaken as a problem but could be an asset later to many types of career choices.) My parents had made me a bed in the back of the car because it was a long drive and my father had to be at the airport early. Dad was driving the car, my brother was sitting behind him, and my sister was behind my mother. My mother was wearing a nice yellow summer dress and scarf. As we pulled up to the gate, Dad pulled over to the side of a fence where you could see the planes. I remember looking at them and wondering which one he would be on. I remember being overcome by an intense fear that Daddy was leaving to go somewhere that wasn't safe. I remember wrapping my arms around him and smelling his fresh uniform and his shaving cream scent. I was thinking to myself that I was afraid, but I could not articulate that feeling. "Daddy, I love you," I said. "I love you, too, honey; now you be a good girl for your mom and grandma," he told me. (I did strive to do exactly that, although at times it would be difficult.) I can still feel the tears well up in my eyes and my heart sink when I think about this feeling of losing my dad, perhaps forever. I loved my dad probably more than he will ever know. He was someone I never understood completely, but somehow I seemed to know just exactly what he was thinking, almost as if we were kindred spirits.

While my father was gone, my mother spent endless amounts of time playing the piano and singing. I remember watching her in wonderment. Though my spoken language was delayed, something very amazing happened. Mom would play the piano, and I would listen. "That's it, honey, just listen to Mommy." She would sing along with her playing. "You can do this, I've heard you sing before, honey; just give it a try." In this case, trying was quite easy for me; I would listen so intently, so passionately. The melody and the words fit together somehow; even today, they still discuss my ability to memorize and sing nursery rhyme songs in perfect tune. I would stand proudly next to that piano, singing each song from memory and learning it in just a few attempts. This was possibly my first clue that I had a gift, and my parents' first clue that I was unique. These gifts, though tough to recall when the pain was evident and negative events would occur, would eventually be one reason for my resilience.

While we were living in California, I reached other developmental milestones. I began to develop friendships, and as I began to be compared with others it caused havoc on my self-esteem. I noticed early on that I was somehow different from other children. I had a cousin, Cathy, who was only 9 months younger than I was.

She was outgoing, cute, and very verbal. I always felt awkward around her. Somehow, even when I was 3½ years old, I felt that my clumsiness was noticed and that my lack of verbal expression was less than adequate. I felt that Cathy was always treated differently than me. I felt she was noticed more. I felt she was better than I was. I'll never forget how I felt when I was compared to her. It seemed that Cathy always did what she was told; she napped when she was told, she ate what was put in front of her, and she went to bed when she was told. I remember her parents when I'd go to her house, even as a young girl, treating me in what today I would describe as a condescending, patronizing way. I was treated as if I was "slow." In looking back now, I think it was my personality; perhaps it annoyed people. I was always too busy; I asked too many questions and interrupted too much. Cathy always teased me about not remembering things, not saying the right things. It only got worse over the years, but I pretended to like everything about her. It wasn't polite to tell people you were hurting because of a little teasing. But I was hurting. It's painful to be different in this way. It is even more painful to have "invisible problems" and not even know how or why you are different.

Please don't misunderstand; I adored my cousin—she was my friend. Looking back, it was clearly a childhood love-hate relationship. My grandmother watched us both while my mother, aunt, and uncle worked. We had such fun, rolling balls down the long hall of our two-family flat, running in the yard, having lunch at the little table with Grandma, and being very mischievous. We kept that wonderful lady quite busy. I am sure Grandma looked forward to nap time; even Cathy looked forward to nap time. I couldn't bear to think about it, however. I would lie there staring at the ceiling. It was around that time period that I began to learn how to control my overactive behavior, act like a nice little girl, and avoid being spanked. I knew it was easier to please those around me than not to, an early sign that I was already developing strong abilities, despite my chaotic mind, in learning to read nonverbal cues. I also was developing strong intuitions. Somehow even at a very early age, I felt I was unique, not typical, although I did not understand why. Even when I was given my bottle (which I kept until I was 4 years old), it didn't relax my mind. I kept turning and turning. My habit of lying there picking all the fuzz from the blanket and the stuffed animals became a way of calming myself when I was thinking faster than I could deal with, which I kept doing until grade school. Of course later I picked up other bad habits to replace those.

I remember it was at this time that I began to hear the record player in my head telling me, "You're really dumb, you're stupid. Just look at yourself and look at Cathy; maybe if you were more like her, then others would like you and want you around more. That's it, try to be more like her." Even as a young child my self-esteem was being dramatically affected; children do start to self-evaluate at a young age. I wonder how many children with hidden disabilities learn at a very young age that they are not a "good fit" in society?

It was in California where I began to feel the pains of childhood ignorance, where I first believed I was being treated like an outsider. The most vivid memory was when Cathy invited another cousin to come over to our house. Even though they were both younger than me, I felt like the younger, more inept child. That particular day we were outside in the front lawn with my tricycle and my horse that had wheels. When Janet stopped by, Cathy switched gears completely; she was now Janet's buddy, and I was the third wheel. Janet jumped on my horse, Cathy on my tricycle, and away they went. I remember not really knowing what to do. I was left alone; they did not return to share their friendship with me. I watched them whisper to each other, look at me, and continue to laugh and play. I never knew what they were saying, but I felt lonely and isolated. I was living in a world of confusion.

Confusion is the best way to describe what I felt, and it occurred everywhere. It was beginning to overwhelm my life. I couldn't explain it then, but I remember one specific event—going to a circus. I was so angry at all the noise, the crowds; I hated the clowns, the tightrope walkers. I couldn't keep focused on anything. It was as if the room was spinning. I remember getting an ill feeling, and it wasn't from the cotton candy. It was the commotion; I know that now, and to this day, I cannot stand public events or places with a lot of stimulation. Even the sounds of crowds when they are constantly cheering cause me much irritation.

I can only imagine how confusing this must have been to my parents. "Mom, where are the clowns?" I would ask my mother. "There, honey, right in front of you," she would say, pointing. But still, I did not see them. I could only see the lights, hear the loud noise and movement. I realized even then my inability; finding things in a room filled with too many stimuli was nearly impossible. I retreated into my own space in my mind: a kind of coping strategy. All my parents wanted to do was give me a surprise, to take me to the circus as a treat, and for me it was pure torture.

I remember the world and feeling as if I did not belong. Nothing seemed to make sense, but I was a people-pleaser; I learned early on that it was easier to pretend than to complain. No one would be angry with me when I would pretend; so hiding the pain was more socially acceptable. What a strange lesson to learn at such a young age. So how do I describe this confusion in detail? I guess the best way to describe this to you is that it is like being in a funhouse with strange mirrors; lights; slanted floors; moving walls; spinning objects; and sudden, loud noises. You step into this funhouse and your whole world is altered. You become lost. For a while it's fun, but imagine what it would be like being trapped in this funhouse every day, each day trying to make sense of your surroundings. I wonder how many people would get used to it. For me, this was my everyday world. At this time I could not explain this experience to others; it is only now that can I put into words how this felt, and it felt horrible. I felt "off," but it was I who was strange. How sad for a child of 4 to know what it is like to be strange. It makes me yearn for the ability to go back in time, to grab hold of me, to hug me and say, "It's all right . . . You are different, but it's okay to be different. You're not dumb, you're not crazy, you're just you."

During this early developmental stage my hyperactivity, inattention, and agitation, combined with my delayed language and paradoxical abilities and weaknesses, were not enough to signal to my family that I needed some help. The information network on hidden disabilities was not then what it is now. Parents did what they could, but without the appropriate support or accurate information they couldn't possibly understand these complications and the long-term effects these problems would have on my life. They thought I would just one day outgrow it, catch up with everyone else. Would it have made a big difference anyway if I had been diagnosed early? The benefit would, perhaps, have been early intervention. Then again, back in the sixties, early diagnosis could have meant that I would have been placed in a situation with others unlike myself, children who had behavior problems or mild mental retardation. So many errors can be made when diagnosing a young child. I think that if my parents had had the opportunity to find accurate information like we have today, perhaps they would have kept a journal of my behavior. I am sure they would have found appropriate help for me. Perhaps given the time it was better that they thought I was just "slow" and different; it may have been what allowed me to adapt. So I progressed on into elementary school, still just a bit "slow," very impulsive, having trouble using appropriate words to express myself, and feeling different.

INSIGHTS AND INTERVENTIONS
by Larry B. Silver, M.D.

The invisible disabilities Veronica has are due to a variation on how her brain is "wired." They are chronic (present from birth) and pervasive in nature (present throughout each day). It is not surprising that she describes them as present during her preschool years.

Veronica's book is full of "if onlys." If only these clear signs of disability had been recognized early and addressed. If only the professionals around her had recognized her problems rather than criticizing her problems. If only her parents were informed of her problems rather than being told that *she* was the problem.

The first clue of her language disability and probably of her language-based learning disabilities that would be diagnosed later was her language delay. As she writes, "It wasn't until it was time for me to start communicating that the concerns began." Her parents were concerned but received the usual feedback: "Don't worry, she will outgrow it." (My plea to physicians and other professionals is this: Never, never say someone has a developmental delay that will go away unless enough testing has been done to establish this view. It is a convenient way to respond to a worried parent but it is often the reason why parents don't seek further tests.) Veronica did not talk until she was 3 years old, and even after this her vocabulary was limited. This should have been an indication to someone to investigate further.

The second clue of a language disability is when a child begins to speak and it becomes apparent that she or he is having difficulty receiving and processing language, organizing thoughts, finding the right words, and expressing language. This can be seen in Veronica's narrative: She notes that she experienced such receptive and expressive language difficulties at age 3 as she began to talk. Throughout this book she describes difficulties in following and understanding what is said and in finding the right thoughts and words to express herself.

Veronica says little about her motor coordination problems in this section of her book; however, she does mention her clumsiness. At this point it would have been too early to recognize a learning disability. Later she notes that she had difficulty even in preschool forming and learning her letters and numbers.

From Veronica's earliest years, *attention-deficit/hyperactivity disorder* (ADHD) is apparent. She gives many examples of being hyperactive, distractible, and impulsive. She was constantly moving. Her parents and others did not understand these behaviors as being linked to her hidden disabilities. Their responses were critical and often punitive. She worked hard at controlling her overactive behavior and to act like a "nice little girl" to avoid being spanked. Veronica gives many examples of being distracted by both sounds and visual stimuli. She often experienced a sensation common to many children with distractibility: sensory overload. Her responses at the circus of being confused and overstimulated were perceived as inappropriate. Yet, her feelings were real and uncontrollable to her. Veronica's impulsivity led to her interrupting, speaking out, and exhibiting risky behaviors before thinking. Playing with fire and climbing the ladder both illustrate this impulsive behavior.

Because Veronica was misunderstood, she was left with only one conclusion: "There must be something wrong with me." How sad it is to hear about a child, not yet 5 years old, thinking such painful thoughts about herself. This chapter is full of instances where she describes herself as being dumb, stupid, and bad. Friends and many adults rejected her. As she says, "It is painful to be different…and not even know how or why you are different." Later she talks of the pain of being treated like an outsider. It is difficult to read her story and not to feel her confusion and pain.

2

BEHIND THE SCHOOLYARD FENCE

ELEMENTARY SCHOOL YEARS

"Veronica daydreams
too much. I know
she could do better
if she
would just
pay attention."

When you're a little girl, you are expected to act like a little lady. I heard this so many times growing up that today, just typing the words gives me the shivers. I'll never forget those early years of my life; I'll never forget the way I felt each day that I went to school. Although I cannot remember the events of each day, I can remember the overwhelming pain and the nightmares that began and followed me into adulthood. I hated school. Not because I was unmotivated or uninterested in learning; actually, I wanted more than anything to learn. Instead, school was a place of misery, a place of solitary internal confinement. For 13 years, from when I was 5 until I was 18, school was a torture chamber. That is a very long sentence to serve for having a hidden disability.

By the time I entered elementary school, we had moved to Virginia. I began to talk more, so much so that it was as if I had been born talking. I also got a new nickname from my dad, "the Mouth"! I really had forgotten that nickname, but he reminded me recently. He said, "You just had this constant running of the mouth, always talking." Mom said I was making up for lost time because I didn't talk much prior to turning 3. I was still having a lot of difficulty with word usage, calling things by the wrong word, mixing up information, and mixing up the delivery of sentences in general.

True to my nickname, whenever we were together, especially in confined spaces, I would start "speed talking." Car trips were the best. All along the road I would have multiple questions to ask and comments to make, no matter how abruptly, and I did not care who was speaking. "Hey Dad, why are there so many trees?" "Hey Mom, can we stop and get a drink?" "Where was it you said we were going?" Almost anything we would pass would trigger the questions. Once we drove past a cemetery and my question shocked everyone in the car. "Mom, when people die and get put in a box, do they put them in on their tummy or on their back?"

Mom answered, "On their back. Why do you ask such a funny question?"

"Mom, promise me when I die, you have them put me on my tummy. I can't sleep on my back." Everyone laughed, but I was serious. I couldn't *not* say something; it wouldn't stay in my head. Why, they even offered me money to keep quiet, but I never made any; I couldn't do it.

All of this talking was funny, at least some of the time. I was the entertainer, but at a price; for every entertainer there is always a critic. Sometimes critics can help a person, and in my case, my favorite critic, Cathy, helped me to see something I was doing that could have become a major point of teasing from other kids.

"Veronica," she said, "why do you do that?"

"Do what?" I replied.

"Mouth the words you say after you finish talking. You say the whole thing right back with your mouth but no words come out. You even do it when I say something—you mouth back what I say."

"I do?" I said, shocked at her comment.

"Yes, and it is very strange." *Strange.* I had another reason to withdraw around kids. I took to heart that what she observed was weird, odd, and I reflected on that and made a strong effort not to do that anymore. It was difficult; it was as if I needed tape to close my mouth, and for years it would be a problem I had to constantly work on.

Although communication was a problem, there were areas where I succeeded. In reflecting on my early elementary years, I can recall other positive major developmental milestones. One that was never a problem was my ability to ride a bike, a two-wheeler bike. My dad taught me in the back yard, on the grass. He didn't want me to fall on the pavement. I took right off. It was probably the easiest thing I learned with the exception of the nursery rhyme songs I had been able to memorize at the age of 4. The wonderful feeling was so overwhelming. I remember singing in my head as I gained speed.

We must look for positive memories in our childhoods, no matter how many or how few; they are like building blocks to our success. It would be easy to focus only on what was wrong in my life, but even at this young age, I was able to reflect on what I did well. It is critical for a parent to help a child find what things he or she does well. A child knows all too well what he or she doesn't do well; human beings, for that matter, are more inclined to find what is wrong with them before they focus on what is right. That, my friends, is something we all can identify in ourselves all too quickly!

Parents, family members, or teachers can always find something that is positive to comment on to a child, even if it is just how well he or she rides a bicycle. For a child, riding a bike for the first time is a big deal, and if the child rides it well, he or she can feel competent in this area, especially if someone points out this skill. It was a good thing that I could ride a bike so well; after all, I couldn't even tie my shoes at the age of 6, and I wouldn't learn to do so until I was almost 8 years old. It gave me some self-confidence at a time I would need it the most. Soon, I would begin my formal education, and once I did, I was going to learn just what life is like when you have something fundamentally different with the way you learn, process, communicate, and interact.

So off I went to begin my educational career. Like most kids, I was nervous but excited. Kindergarten then was much different than it is today; we were allowed to play a lot more, we did not start reading anything except the letters of the alphabet, and we counted up to 10. Of course, as simple as that may be, for me it was an early sign of trouble. My letters would get "messed up." To me, a *p* looked like a *q,* a *d*

Veronica in Kindergarten

16

looked like a *b,* and, what was that again, does *t* come before *s,* or is it before *r*? But many children had that same problem, so no big deal, right? Wrong. Wrong because there were many other signs before and during this time that things were not quite right. With every weakness comes a strength, however, and for what I lacked in academics, I did not lack in imagination. I remember playing out stories, fantasies in my mind. I could do this for what seemed all day. I would create adventures, travel to wonderful places in my head. I'd sit on a spring horse at recess and pretend to run off into the sunset. I could see it clearly, in color—the horse, the sun, the desert—everything was clear. Then I would notice I was the only one left on the playground. Usually, a very annoyed teacher would make this known to me. "Veronica, come now, the others are waiting for you. Veronica, what are you doing? Hurry now." Little did we know then that others would continue to wait on me; I would show my slowness as time went by in very obvious ways. Overall, however, this first half-year was a good one for me, but of course, it was time to move on again.

Next, we moved from Virginia to Colorado where I began kindergarten again. I don't recall a lot about it, except that it was a long walk to and from school. The walk to school was fine, but it was at that time that I didn't really want to go; it was getting harder, and the teacher wasn't as nice as the one at my old school. She noticed things about my clumsiness, my awkwardness, my inattention, and all the "unnecessary questions" I would ask. Teachers sometimes have a way of making children feel stranger than they already feel. The power a teacher has in developing a young mind is incredible; in fact, most teachers, if you think about it, spend more time with a child in a week than the child's own family does. Such power can be viewed either as a curse or a blessing. In my case it was often a curse, so much so, that I would begin to retreat into my mind. I was stuffing down so much pain that it had to get out somehow, and for me it escaped in the form of an evolving dream.

Sometimes we have dreams that continue, kind of like a miniseries. For me, I would have these recurring dreams at times of change. A family move would usually trigger them, but some of them came between the moves. I'll never forget these dreams. At first they were horrible. I dreamed of a monster chasing me, trying to harm me. The monster was grotesque. It was always lagging behind; it was clueless, lost, and it needed to be noticed, like me. I never saw its face. As a child I'd try to escape reality every time we moved—to leave the monster behind. It was only much later, after years of therapy to undo my damaged self-esteem, that I learned why I could not leave it behind. The monster was the "stupid" kid— my poor self-image of *me.* When I started first grade, I was at a new school and a new house, which was located in military base housing in Denver. Either fortunately or unfortunately, I was one of the prettiest little girls in the class, always polite, always compliant. My parents brought me up to respect my elders, to be kind to others, and to always—under every circumstance—do what I was told. So I did; I learned that by being silent, by smiling, and by looking up at the teacher at the appropriate times, I could avoid problems. It worked well; I could hide all the confusion (as long as they didn't ask me questions). It was at this time that I learned that being polite and "cute" would help me survive. It is easier for a child to survive in school if she is a people pleaser. What I didn't know was that this would also come close to destroying me in years to come, and that getting past the destruction this caused would take incredible internal strength.

I was in the first grade when I noticed that I didn't understand directions, regardless of how they were presented, either oral or written. Fortunately for me, I had a wonderful teacher that year; I worked very hard because I loved her. She was gentle, caring, and soft-spoken. First grade was more demanding than kindergarten, and we were required to "print" letters. I was ready for the challenge: Surely I could do this well. But I remember how hard it was to form those letters. When I would print, I would press hard on those pages with all of my might, holding my pen like a pitchfork, to try to create a picture-perfect letter. Oh, the pain in my hand was great, but the praise I would get from her—the love she had in her eyes—was all that I needed to keep going. "That's very good, Veronica, you're trying very hard, what nice effort you are making," I remember her saying.

"Thank you," I would respond lovingly. A child needs to know the kindness of healthy love. She may well have been my first "charismatic adult," a term I learned from a presentation given by Dr. Robert Brooks, a person known as "the self-esteem teacher." He defines this as an adult who leads a child with understanding, belief, empathy, and concern—someone who would never hurt a child but instead provides the child with warmth and support. These are the people who foster resilience in children, and God knows, I would need a lot of that in years to come.

It was in first grade that we also began to read, and like most first-graders, we started with *Dick and Jane* books. Little did my teacher know that I was memorizing the books, not really reading the words. The words seemed so similar, the word *was* could have been *saw* and the word *them* could have been *they,* and *then* was often *the.* It was all so confusing: I would feel anxious when it was my turn to read, when I had to recall what words came next, and when I had to try to read the words and get them right. Even today I ache thinking about it. There was never a safe time to relax. I would count the number of kids in each row who would read before me, listening intently to what they said. I could only pray that the row order would be kept; if my concentration was broken by a new name being called, a bell ringing, a student dropping a pencil or tapping a desk, it was all but lost. I would tell myself that there were just a few words on the page, I would just need to listen carefully and look at the first letter for a clue. "See Dick run, see Jane run, see Spot run." Sometimes I would read words on a page that didn't even exist (I would make them up based on the first letters of words). I had trouble telling time; after all, it's pretty hard to understand the differences between a minute hand and an hour hand when "big" and "little" mean the same.

Even if I did mess up, it was acceptable, at least to my parents and to the teacher, because after all I was still only in the first grade. I would improve, they thought; I just needed a little extra help. It was good that they felt this way, because I didn't feel too good about myself. I certainly didn't need any negative reinforcement from them. I was hard enough on myself.

One day a note went home to my parents; it was time for the girls to join the Brownie troop. It sounded like fun; maybe there I would get to do things I was good at. They talked a lot about arts and crafts and nature. I liked all of those things, so I asked if I could join. Mom was pleased; we already had the uniform because my sister had been a Brownie, so off I went to the first meeting. To my surprise we were given a book, and to earn badges I had to read the book and do what it told me to do. "Can't I escape this struggle?" I thought to myself. "Isn't there anyplace I can go to get away from this?"

Over the next month, I hated going to Brownies. There were games with instructions to follow and rules that I would always forget. One day I had to join a group to play a game that required reading some cards. I would have to figure it out, not miss a beat. Unfortunately for me, I had a doubly embarrassing experience; I could not figure it out, and the other girls were getting very upset with me. I remember them saying, "She's going too slow; she is going to mess us up." I was working so hard on trying to keep up that my need to use the girls' room became less important and I had an accident, right in front of everyone. I still remember the faces of the girls, smirking and laughing. Sometimes I felt like God didn't like me much—that one bad thing seemed always to lead to another. After that, I never returned to Brownies.

I remember talking to my grandma one day after school. I came home, and she was preparing our evening meal. Grandma noticed that I was upset, and she asked how my day had gone.

"Not good, Grandma."

"Why not, honey?" she asked.

"Grandma," I replied, "I'm not good in school. I'm dumb—other kids read and do other things better than me."

She looked at me with concern in her eyes. She stopped what she was doing, looked at me, and said, "It will be all right, honey, there is something special about you. One day you will know what it is and you will be the best you can be." Grandma probably had no idea what those words meant to me, *I had something special.* Although I didn't know what it was, I believed her and would repeat those words for years to come. Of course, the help I needed was beyond academics. I was bright yet I knew I was different. I could see the other kids learning, and I felt that I was not. It hurt to see that I was "weird"—unlike the other kids. The kids noticed and so did I. As a result I started my academic career already feeling bad about myself. Already, in first grade I was going from not liking myself to hating myself.

School let out for the summer and not soon enough; we were ready for a vacation. But there really was no escape from my feeling that I was stupid. When you have a child with learning disabilities (LD), problems don't occur only at school. Perhaps if that were the case, the child might experience some better feelings in other environments. For me, my "differentness" was obvious in all areas; my disabilities were substantial and affected how I functioned in society as well. If you think about learning, it would be easy to understand how a child might shy away from activities such as games. Games require reading, sometimes math, writing, problem solving, and communicating. Back before we had compact disc players, video games, or computers, games were heavily language-based. For my older, wiser siblings, playing games with me meant winning easily, especially when play money was involved. They would simply tell me that bigger-sized money was worth more, so nickels and pennies were worth more than dimes. Unfortunately, we didn't have quarters to play with, which was too bad for me. I was always very gullible; I would believe anything anyone would tell me. I would do anything I was told. I just couldn't decipher between good and bad. And forget the typical car games, which of course included reading the signs along the way. The license plate game was nothing but frustrating for me; I would just lay in the back and sing to myself. Thank God my brother and sister couldn't sing; it was the one thing I could do better than they could, which Mom and Dad made very clear to both of them whenever they would begin teasing me.

By the time second grade rolled around, I began to get anxious; but what was I anxious about? I was afraid I'd fail, and I wanted so much to do well. Even though I had had a good year in first grade, it was a struggle, a constant effort, and I had already observed how much faster the other kids were catching on. They got their work done before me; they answered questions I couldn't. Then I would start in on the self-actualization: "I am smart, I really am." Then my mind would scream, "No, I'm really not!" Sadly, I did not get a teacher like I had the previous year. Though many children did seem to love this new teacher, she, for whatever reason, did not have the patience that my first-grade teacher had. She did not like to wait for me. It was, after all, second grade: Time to grow up! I wanted to please her, but I just didn't seem to have the ability. Without encouragement and unconditional love, I wanted to give up. Why try?

It seemed to me that whatever I did was not good enough. Notes went home to my parents; homework went home because I couldn't finish it in class. And if school wasn't bad enough, I had to go to my safe haven and be reminded all over how very stupid I was. I wonder if people give consideration to what it must be like for a child to struggle all day in school, only to come home and face THE HOMEWORK. Both my father and mother would sit up until what seemed midnight (though it wasn't) trying to drill the math and reading into my head. My father (who I think was my genetic link to my learning problems) had little patience, and out of his concern, I am certain he became highly frustrated. He would explain over and over again, "Veronica, you have five apples, you take one away and what do you have?" My response varied from, "What did you say?" to "I think one." I was so confused. Most nights he would just give me the answers and push me up to bed. I was so sad to have disappointed my dad. I loved him; I wanted to be like my brother and sister, I just couldn't seem to get it right. No child wants to fail. There is always a reason behind the failure.

Every night it was a battle to sleep, I kept thinking about my day, my homework. The nightmare of the monster pursuing me would begin, represented perhaps in different ways each time, but with the same message of incompetence and sadness. The nightmares that caused me to hide under my covers, the sweat rolling off my skin, crying out loud inside, "Please come rescue me, somebody help me!" —it was more than I could handle. I hated my life; for the first time I can remember I wanted to die and I was only 7. It was the first time I felt like giving up; I felt I was worthless.

Just like the games, my disabilities would show up everywhere. I noticed that my language and my memory were different than that of others. I began to evaluate what other people were able to do and to ask myself why I couldn't do it. During meals at home, while my family members would talk about different things, I would try desperately to tell a story. I would use the wrong word or give the wrong fact and immediately get corrected by my much smarter, or maybe I should say sharper, sister or brother. It was so frustrating to me to know what I wanted to say but not be able to get it out. I thought that I had the facts right, but somehow the information got mixed up. I'll never forget one night at the dinner table trying to explain about watching the Apollo moon mission lift off on television at school. I was so excited about what I had seen. I jumped into the middle of a conversation (which I regularly did) and announced my knowledge of how fast and how far they were going. Upon my quote, everyone laughed; I was so devastated. My brother explained "You're wrong as usual!" These words "you're wrong" —I can't tell you how many times I heard them. My instant reaction was one of anger: "No, I am not wrong!" Well, truth be told, I was a little wrong; I had the numbers mixed up. The sequence was wrong. This wasn't uncommon for me at all. It hurt so much sitting there, feeling small, dumb, and a misfit in a family of really smart people. I was the idiot. I had not yet learned to be quiet. And, of course, a strong message was sent to me when this happened: If you don't talk to people, they won't know you are dumb. This was a lesson I carried a bit too far, and I was caught in what could have been a horrible tragedy in my life and my family.

It was when I was so very young that I learned the world is unforgiving of ignorance. I believed that my lack of understanding — the way I interpreted the world — was something everyone would notice. I had to work very hard to hide that I was different. It wasn't that people were mean; actually, they were just uninformed. They did the best they could, and with me, their best was probably to my benefit. After all, it was the early seventies, and although learning disabilities were a known problem to some, to many *learning disability* was not a common phrase. My parents were hard-working people; information was not as available then as it is now, and schools were not as tuned in either. What my parents did do was help me to survive, help me with homework. They brought me up in a highly structured environment, teaching me morals, ethics, and general dignity not only for myself, but for others. These skills taught me more than I learned in any one math or reading class I had as a child. My biggest problem at this age was that I had this overwhelming fear of not knowing why I was different than everyone else, very different. I did not know how I fit in, or if I would ever fit in. I'm not sure I really knew the answer to that until recently.

You know how a second grader knows that she does not "fit in?" From observing and comparing myself to other kids, I came to see myself as dumb, and the feeling was overwhelming. I just wanted to be liked. I didn't know when I wasn't welcome; well actually, deep down inside I did — I was just hoping for a miracle. I was the perfect victim to be bullied and teased by other kids. My strange yet quiet behavior was obvious to the bullies. My inability to remember where the restroom was, my losing my way to the bus, my lack of ability to keep up in class, it was all noticed, and I was easy prey. One day in particular comes to mind when I was invited to a party. All of the kids in my class were invited. The girl having the party never talked to me. As a matter of fact, on many occasions she made fun of me in class. She had an older brother who also went to our school. I was to ride a bus home with her on the day of the party; I was nervous but excited. I was standing near the bus holding the present when the girl's older brother approached me. He started trying to confuse me, telling me I had to be on another bus. All this was arranged so that I would miss the party because the birthday girl didn't want me there. The boy grabbed my schoolbooks from me and yelled that I was too stupid to use them anyway. "Hey, you stupid girl, why are you at this school anyway? All the kids say you're dumb, you shouldn't be here, you should be in a school for retards." He left the scene laughing, and I missed the bus. Tears streamed down my face. It was that single event and more I would experience in school and in life that would cause such emotional harm; it devastated me. I was getting tired of pretending I was happy. I couldn't fake it anymore. Everyone knew I was stupid.

The pain of being in second grade and my pervasive belief that I was stupid had become so real that I would even harm myself physically to escape reading out loud or taking a test. I remember one time in second grade, I had it all planned out: I would sit in front of the school building in a very unnoticeable manner, slam my wrist hard against the fence, and tell the teacher on duty that I fell so that I could go home. I remember being proud of my accomplished task—a very badly bruised and swollen wrist. I didn't hurt myself, really, but it was better than taking a spelling test I knew I would fail. As I write this I realize just how desperate I was to not fail, even at the age of 7. All I can do is cry from this memory. It is as if I was living it all over again, only this time, I allow myself to understand why it hurts so much. I remember the feelings of desperation and isolation, the utter fear of being called on in class; the terror was too much. I didn't try to lie or to explain it away. But unfortunately, the insecurity and the sadness I felt created an even bigger risk for me than school failure. I would have to cross another event that would leave lifelong scars.

It was on a playground of a schoolyard near our house that I lost more of myself. I learned a horrible lesson that would become just one more hurdle for me to climb over. After school, my brother and I would frequently go to the school not far from our house to play. That day, he had made arrangements to leave me alone so he could be with his friends, not an uncommon thing for an older sibling to do. After all, what could happen? It was daylight, and it was a schoolyard.

My brother and I got to the swings and he told me, "I want to go play—I will give you anything you want if you will stay here until I get back." Anything? I thought that was a good deal. So off he went. Soon, a grown man approached me. He looked nice enough, but Mom and Dad said never to talk to strangers. I was alone on the playground. No one else was anywhere to been seen. I felt strange, so I put my head down hoping he would go away. He didn't. "Hey there, looks like you were left here, are you okay?" I nodded. "Well, do you mind if I sit on this swing?" he said. Again, I nodded in an "I don't care" kind of way. "Do you live near here?" he asked. "Hey, it's okay, your parents probably told you not to talk to a stranger. That's what I tell my kids." Well, that was the first level of trust; I fell for it—a stranger wouldn't have kids, he must be okay—but still I was uncomfortable. I also knew I was alone.

"My brother will be coming to get me soon," I stated.

"Oh, how old is your brother?"

"He's 12. He went to get a pencil so we could work on our home-work; he'll be back soon," I answered. As with any pedophile, he was very good at picking up on just how to get a child on his side.

"What is your homework?" he asked.

"Math," I said with a less than excited tone in my voice.

"Well, math is my best subject; could you use some help?" Though I said no, he pressed on: "My daughter is about your age. What are you working on—subtraction?"

"Yes," I responded.

"Hey, I can sit right here and give you some tips while you wait." I guess I figured that that would be okay; he was here anyway, so carefully I picked up my book. He moved his swing closer to mine and began to instruct me; he seemed so nice— maybe this guy was okay?

After a while he suggested that we find a park bench to sit on back in the woods. The swings weren't very comfortable. "Okay, I guess that is okay." In my mind, he hadn't been bad. Besides, strangers that are bad are mean looking. He wasn't, and he had kids. How sad—my naiveté. As we were walking toward the woods, he placed his hand on my lower back and began running his hand up and down my back.

I don't remember much after that—it is mostly blank in my memory. Years later, I would discover the truth about that day, but until that time it became a suppressed memory. I do remember my brother's voice, as clear as a bell, "Veronica!" I emerged slowly; he looked at me, I looked at him, and we began to walk back home, "Don't tell anyone, Veronica, we'll get into lots of trouble." I only regret not telling so that another child would not be harmed. It was bad enough that two were already affected; my brother had to deal with terrible guilt for leaving me behind.

From that day forward, my life had changed even more. Now my problems were not just about learning: Now I did not trust. Fortunately for me, I was able to disassociate (most would consider that a bad thing, but in this case it probably saved me) from the experience. It was time to move on, to become even stronger and more resilient.

In reflecting about my childhood, I don't think my parents ever knew the pain I felt overall. Years later, when I was an adult, they learned, and I know they felt pain for me as a child. But they were exceptional in that they had decided to see mostly my strengths, the good things, my resilience, and my interest in pleasing people. To them this was a gift and they were right, but inside I was trying to hide, to not let anyone know how dumb I really was, and what happened on the playground made me feel even more stupid. I began to realize that in a world that really didn't care much about others, most people were self-serving. Of course, those words were not ones I used; it was more of a realization that I had. I was angry that people didn't see that I was lost, hurting, and in pain. After all, weren't adults supposed to take care of kids? It hurt so badly inside. Why didn't people see it, feel it, react to it? Why did people just get annoyed and make me feel worse? I was already feeling as bad as anyone could.

We left Denver, and not too soon for me. When the move was announced, I was thrilled. It was time to move on. Maybe the next place would be different. Maybe I would find peace. After all, it had worked for a while before, why not this time? I can start over, I thought. Maybe in the next school, the next town, I'll be smart. Maybe?!

We arrived in St. Louis the summer before third grade. I was so excited, but during our first night in the new house, the dream recurred. The monster had made it to Denver just as we left; it was angry that I had escaped. I was relieved; I had not been caught.

It was during the next few years that I would learn to select friends who were kind, caring, giving, and smart. That is when I met my best friend—Carolyn. I'll never forget her. For years, until adulthood, we stayed in touch. She probably never knew how much she helped me survive through 3 years of elementary school.

By the time I had started the fall session, I had developed a strong-enough relationship with Carolyn and a couple of other kids that I was confident I would make it. I had a pretty nice teacher; she looked a little like my mother so I felt comfortable with her. Safety allowed me to have an open mind. I knew I was different, but perhaps here with this teacher, I could do better. I would push on to succeed. People at the school discovered at the beginning of the year that my reading, writing, grammar, math, and attention skills were a problem, but my teachers and parents didn't label it anything, except "she's a bit slow." It was pretty obvious that there were problems; my homework was nearly perfect because I had either cheated or had my family do it for me; but my day-to-day schoolwork was a mess: failed tests, class projects, all were in disarray. A classic example of a warning sign was that I still could not tell time. As I mentioned before, I had some trouble with the minute and hour hands; well into the third grade and even all through fifth grade, I could not tell time unless it was on the hour or half hour; nothing in between made any sense. I used to sit for hours with this child's toy called Hickory Dickory Dock (a Fisher Price toy) and work with the clock to try any method I could to learn it; even my parents made many efforts. Nothing worked.

I was placed in the low reading group. Oh sure, it had its name like they all do. You'd think school personnel would figure out that kids aren't as clueless as they think they are. Everybody knows that a rabbit is faster than a gopher. I was glad by this point to be in the "slow" group; I knew I was slow. It didn't mean I didn't want to be in the fast group. I longed for it, I dreamed about it, like it was an Academy Award. But I also knew I would never survive it, so why try? I remember studying the kids in the other group, comparing myself to them. What was different about me? We all looked the same, talked the same, and we were about the same age. I quickly came to the conclusion that it was simply because they were smart and I was dumb; that was the reality of my life.

Of course, what made this observation even more complete was my lack of math skills. To this day I can only do adding, sub-tracting, and multiplication (okay, some division). But in all honesty, I am amazed I even got through school because my skills in this academic area were so severely limited. I guess the most profound example I can give you is the one when the teacher gives the lesson on the blackboard. You have all experienced it: The teacher works the problems on the board and then the students work them at their desks. This seems simple enough, but to a third-grade child who watches the teacher solve the problem like lightning and who then has to try to understand where the numbers go—in what order and why—it is overwhelming. In my case, no one explained the steps, not in the way I learn. Why couldn't someone number the process and let me use an example of how I arrived at my answer through the use of a sequence sheet in the test or even during homework? Why couldn't they let me have a sample formula with the steps written out and explained? Would it have been so difficult to excuse me from having to go up to the blackboard with my back to the students and work the problem? I was angry with the teacher, although she was just doing her job. In the mind of a child who is struggling day in and day out, wondering, "Why don't they notice I am not getting this?" resentment does begin to set in. How could an adult who teaches kids not recognize that each time I was asked to do this type of task, I failed—in front of everyone?

I remember one specific incident; three of us were called up to do "long division." I was shaking, "Oh God, please let me trip on something, hit my head; let the bell ring, please." But no, that did not happen. Instead, I watched over my shoulder; I stood back carefully trying to look like I was analyzing the problem and watched what the other kids were doing closely. Sometimes I could pull this off, but the biggest problem was that I could not remember the multiplication table to do the tasks; it was always wrong. Do you know what it is like to always be wrong in front of 20 people you see *every day*? I wanted to become invisible.

Parents don't always know what goes on with their kids. What I mean is, they may think their child is happy because he or she may laugh hysterically over what might be nothing, or the child may tell them things are great at school and show no signs of anything else. But behind closed doors, that is not always the reality. I remember one time when, for whatever reason, I just couldn't take the feeling of being inadequate anymore. It was this year that my depression began to set in, when I began to overanalyze my world and everyone in it. There was a song many years ago, "The End of the World." I still remember it as if it were yesterday, there I was standing in the shower, saddened by my day of trying to be "normal" and not succeeding. This song came on and the words ripped through me, begging me to cry out. I fell to the floor shuddering in a flood of tears. The words that stunned me that day still stay with me today: "I wake up in the morning and I wonder why ev'rything's [sic] the same as it was—I can't understand, no, I can't understand how life goes on the way it does!" How sad the feeling a child has to have of total emptiness, loneliness, internal rejection. No one else would have to reject me; all on my own I was my worst enemy, and anyone else just justified my pain.

Fortunately, however, my parents discovered that I had a musical talent and I started to play the violin. They had noticed this talent when I was 4; I was able to sing in perfect key all of the words to all of the nursery rhymes my mother taught me, and I could pick out songs one key at a time on the piano. I could never read the notes well. With the type of learning disabilities I had, it was nearly impossible for me to read them fast enough to keep up. But that didn't matter, I was blessed with a wonderful auditory musical memory. I have the ability to hear, learn, and retain music very well. My life was different after this discovery: I had a talent; I could do something better than the other kids could. I was good, I was very good. Oh, if only I had the desire to practice more; I just couldn't get motivated to do it; after all, it was only music class. That doesn't make you smart, it just makes you talented, I told myself. Oh well, I'd say to myself, at least I am talented. Dumb and talented, what an oxymoron. If only the schools would give music equal stature with academics and sports. I wonder how many kids would be in high graces with other kids if musical abilities were looked on with more respect? The students involved in music may even feel better about themselves.

So what did I do to feel good about myself? After all, I could not be in music class all day. So, I began to learn the act of pretending that I could read. Pretending was a big part of my life. I would create stories in my head where I was at the top of the class, the best at softball, anything. In my dreams I was self-assured. I would even daydream in school during my third-grade year. The best place to do this was in a new center that the library had built. I'll never forget it. It was a loft with lots of pillows and beanbag chairs, and it was private. I loved going up there; I would lay down next to a window and pretend to be reading and daydream as long as they would let me. I would imagine music I had heard, what the clouds looked like, what my life would be like when I was grown. Then I would look down at the book, look around the room of kids reading, studying, and talking about what they were learning, and realize it was only a dream. After all, what could I be? I couldn't even keep up with the other kids; I'd have to find a way for someone to take care of me.

Can you imagine what it is like to pretend to be able to read? Oh, what an art form it is. I'd stare at other kids in wonder, at the words on the pages of the book. Why couldn't I read well? Why could everyone else do it so well? You see, I could read simple words. I had memorized a lot of those. The new big words were more difficult, so I listened and problem solved. It wasn't really that hard to develop this skill. Let me explain. Here is a sentence example. The horse ran across the *tundra* with *amazing* speed! Well this should not be hard—I knew these words: The horse ran across the _____ with _____ speed! Okay, so I don't know what kind of land it was, or how incredible the speed was, but I knew it was a horse running with speed. Now, for the problem solving. Chances are these were new words, chances are the teacher was going to repeat them, or someone else in the class would, in either the exact sentence or in a discussion of their definition. I just had to listen very closely. If I wasn't that lucky, it was okay; at least I got the gist of the sentence. Sometimes this worked, sometimes it didn't. When it didn't work, I had to find a really smart kid in class and ask him or her to tell me what (holding my finger to the words) the definition of that word was. Nine times out of ten, it was a snap. People love to look smart. I could still get what I needed, because I was nice, cute. It worked; I could carry on with my hiding.

Again I had learned that people want control; they want to show their ability. I knew *that*, I wanted it myself, I was just too ignorant to do it. So I did learn that I could try harder by having my friends help me with the work. In some twisted way, getting someone else to do your work takes a lot of hard work and creativity. But as I alluded to earlier, people get tired of "helping the dummy." But hey, the system worked. Get an A on homework, fail the test, and you get a C for the class. Ah, yes, I had found a system, and it worked at home, school, and with my friends. I just couldn't let anyone know how angry I was, how stupid I was, and how much I wished I could just disappear. This feeling was overwhelming, a kid knowing she was a fake at such a young age, a little con artist just trying to survive. How I wished I weren't me.

I guess the most important part of these early years was how I learned to manipulate my friends and family into doing my home-work for me. Carolyn was a willing participant, at least for the first year. Year 2 was different; I became annoying, always asking for help. She began to figure it out and I remember developing a fear of trying to come up with the next excuse for why she should help me. "Carolyn, I was working on reading and I began the assign-ment, then I forgot my book. Could I borrow yours? Oh, and so I understand what we are supposed to do, would you mind letting me copy your work? You know we will have a quiz, so would it really cause any harm?" Or, "Carolyn, I was wondering, could you look over my homework and correct it for me?" I came up with endless ideas for recruiting people's help. The few times she rejected me, I would turn to other people: my brother, my dad, my mom, the other girl down the street who would "tolerate me" for favors. All of this manipulation taught me about people, and about myself. Unfortunately, most of what I learned created so much pain

Veronica (center) with brother Anthony (left) and sister Teresa (right)

for me later that turning this negative, maladaptive behavior into a positive one took years of work and reality therapy.

It was these skills and my politeness that made me the perfect child for social promotion to the next grade, not a bad thing when combined with hard work, but it was sticky social promotion in many cases. I was sweet, kind, and always willing to help. Regardless, I continued to learn how to use nonverbal ways to help me survive; I learned how to find a way out of a mess rather eloquently. I learned negotiation skills and skills for reading others, all of which were useful as an adult.

Change is inevitable, however, and I faced a time when social promotion didn't work. It was then that reality hit like a ton of bricks. I remember fifth grade; once again I became overwhelmed by the real world of homework. We were assigned it nightly and expected to know it for verbal interaction the next day. I had to find another way; it wasn't enough for me to sit, smile, and observe. It wasn't enough for me to make excuses for not knowing something, and it wasn't enough for me to offer to help. This teacher thought she had my number, and she made it clear to my parents. "Veronica daydreams too much. I know she could do better if she would just pay attention. She is a pleasant student, very helpful and kind, but that does not get the grades. Homework is fine, but quizzes, tests, and in-class work, well, that is another story." My homework was fine, but only because my friends did it for me or my family helped more than they should have out of concern or personal frustration they were feeling over trying to help and getting nowhere with me. Of course, Mom and Dad had heard all of this before, and, as before, they would begin their long lecture. "We know she daydreams, other teachers have told us this, but we also know that she is trying. We don't know what to do."

"Well, she just lacks discipline and motivation, she needs to be shown that if she does not get busy, it will hurt her later," the teacher said. These were words we already knew to be true, but they were coming from someone who obviously knew nothing about learning disabilities. Was it her fault, or was it the fault of the system? In any case, the conversations would begin at home. "You'd better try harder, you'd better try harder, you'd better try harder!" I was confused, I only wished they knew how hard I *was* trying, and the price I was paying was in having to bribe, manipulate, and lie my way through school. My feelings of disappointment in myself were high; I felt I had let my parents down. They expected improvements and I wasn't making them. They must have felt so out of control. Not having gone through this with my sister or brother; it must have created much concern and sadness.

It was also in fifth grade that I was exposed to what I would call my first realization that even on a social level, I would continue to mess up, miss the "political rules." These political cues that changed everywhere I went would have an impact on me for the rest of my life. Once, I was on the playground. It was cold that day. I couldn't participate in ball games—I wasn't ever coordinated enough—so like all the years before I would find a place to sit, think, or talk to another student. I found an inviting swing but I didn't notice a group of kids close by. Even though they stood there every day I hadn't noticed that this swing "belonged" to the "tough kids," that anyone who sat on those swings was subject to emotional torment or physical trauma.

"Hey kid, get off that swing. Who do you think you are?" they said. I turned and looked at the four of them, much bigger than me.

"What swing is yours?" I asked. I guess they thought I was being smart with them, but I was sincere. "No one was using it— I'm just sitting here," I stated.

"It's not yours, it's ours. No one can use it except us—don't act stupid." Those words again—so painful, so real to me. I got up and walked away. Not because they were getting closer in proximity to me, but because I was about to cry. I couldn't let anyone see that, they'd know it was true. Sadly, that was not the end of it. They later grabbed me and threw me against a brick wall and told me next time it would be worse than this. This harshness was something I internalized as "all me." I could not make the connection that these kids would have done this to anyone else; it was all because I was a reject, the school idiot.

By the end of fifth grade, it was time to move again. Carolyn and I were devastated. My family and I would be leaving from school on the last day, moving to another town. I'll never forget that day. We hugged at the car, I cried, she cried. I thought to myself how dear she was to me. I knew I hadn't been the best friend to her: I had talked her into doing my homework, had her wait on me left and right, and had even ordered her around like a dog at times. I hadn't treated her with the love and kindness she deserved. I realized it was wrong, and I wondered why she cared, but she did.

As we pulled away and she went running after our car, I became hysterical. I had lost my angel, the one person in the world who knew my secret, the one who had gotten me through 3 years of school, she was gone. How did she have so much wisdom for such a young person? Why was she so accepting of me? So many kids had laughed at me, left me alone, but not Carolyn. Did she need me as much as I needed her, or was she just a rare human being I was fortunate enough to find? I worried, would I find another Carolyn at the new school?

Shortly after we moved into the new house, the dream occurred again; the monster was looking for me in St. Louis and again the monster hadn't found me, but it had found my friend Carolyn. I was so scared for her. I knew it was just a dream, but it had to mean something. I just didn't know what. Now I know it found her because I was gone and lost without her help. I did know one thing for sure; I had escaped the monster yet again. This time, however, I was more worried. Dad had retired from the military and was working for a company that would not likely transfer him anywhere else. Here we were to stay. The monster could find me here; it could take over and likely would.

I began sixth grade in public school much like the one in St. Louis, only there wasn't anyone in my class like Carolyn. I would struggle more this year than any other. It was this year I began to be cynical about life in addition to feeling stupid and wanting to disappear. My first round of significant depression began that year. The signs were there, but most people would never have noticed it because I was so good at the art of pretending, even when all I wanted to do was die. You see, I didn't have the support I had gotten from Carolyn. I felt that I had to find a way to make some new friends. I managed to meet one girl in my class who was also new. She was very smart and very beautiful—a future model type. I was so insecure around her, but I began the mission to get her to help me. But unfortunately, she did not buy into my scheme. She was secure enough in herself; she did not have to prove herself to me to secure my friendship, so alone I stayed. I realized I would have to learn another skill. Ah, plagiarism! I knew what I was up against; I had failed so many times already. Now I had to find a way to survive with or without the other kids.

It wasn't hard really; I just found very old books, old encyclopedias, and asked lots of questions. By this time, I was reading words by sight but still I could not comprehend. I got lucky many times by checking the right answers or saying the right thing, but overall the teachers knew something was very wrong. They just chose to mark down that I was lazy, slow, and not very bright. I guess it was evident in everything I did. I completed all of my work more slowly than the other kids did; now in sixth grade my second-grade pace was very obvious. I worked very hard to do all of my work carefully and slowly in an effort to get it right or avoid being called on. I just couldn't bear to walk up to the teacher in front of all of the kids, their eyes on my back looking at me, laughing at me. "Oh, please, God," I'd say to myself, "let me get by just another day; I'll do anything."

It was this year that my teachers informed my parents that I wasn't very intelligent; it wasn't just a matter of being "slow" anymore. Reality hit home and it was time to figure out what to do with me; my parents believed that I would not make it in the traditional school.

As my parents explored their options, they decided to find something I could do well. One thing they knew for sure was that I had musical talent, and lucky for me, we had an organ at home. My parents found an organ teacher, and did I ever learn quickly! This was one of the most important things my parents did for me, and it may have saved my life. The sacrifices they made to get me there—the many drives an hour out of the way to go to the right teacher—helped me develop my skills. My mother was committed to helping me find success even though she was exhausted from working long, hard hours; she made sure I had a way to show my ability. She knew that this was critical, I had to have something to fall back on. I had to find a reason to go on. Of course, my disability would also show up in music. But for what I lacked in the ability to track notes on a page and to remember how to read them, I made up for with my outstanding musical auditory memory that had been evident even when I was just 3 years old.

Despite the positive reinforcement I received from my parents regarding my musical ability, I interpreted their brief comments in a negative way. This was not because I didn't think I was talented but because of their view that I could make music a career. In an attempt to help me see options in my adult life, my parents talked about how I could make good money playing the organ for church, weddings, and funerals. But in my eyes, all I could see was that they were saying I had to do this because I couldn't do anything else. Unfortunately, my parents loving and good intentions frightened me. How could they have known that there wasn't a lot of need for a star organist in the late seventies, and little did they know I hated myself so much because I thought I was dumb that no matter how good I was, I didn't have the courage to try.

How sad to have a talent but no self-esteem! What is the point of having a talent if one can't use it to create opportunities for success, or perhaps link it to another related career? Somehow we often miss this point with our kids. As a society, we need to see how critical self-esteem is for everyone. Being involved in activities can be great for children, but hobbies and sports cannot replace a damaged self-esteem. Still, parents, teachers, and others can create more opportunities for kids to be involved in nontraditional ways, such as volunteering, starting a fund-raising campaign, or starting a club. This encourages kids to do things that allow them to show their abilities in areas outside of academics, and it helps them see how academics and creativity can relate together. In these types of ways, we certainly will enhance our chances of improving, and even developing a stronger sense of ourselves.

Though I had many successes in my sixth-grade year, I also had many awakenings, many painful thoughts, leading to depressive tendencies, abusive behavior, and an emerging pattern of substance abuse. I learned very quickly that drinking a little wine (either when I was allowed to or when I was to clear the table and would suck down everyone's leftovers) made me feel more relaxed. Unfortunately, what I didn't know was that this was a quick fix to a big problem, one that if left ignored would eventually cause even more trauma. I left sixth grade feeling more incompetent, more frustrated than I ever had in my life, though not in the area of music. After all, having it confirmed that I did, indeed, have musical talent was a milestone in my life.

Looking back at those times as I write this book, I reflect on many things, some of which I have chosen to leave out because they would be irrelevant. What is relevant is that it was at this time, in my preteen years, that I began to develop psychological problems. The question we must ask is, were my problems the result of having learning disabilities, were they a result of some emotional issues, or did I have an underlying genetic predisposition to a psychological illness? (Personally, I believe it was a result of all three.) Regardless of the reason, the fact remains that I was still not learning, I was still behind, and I was still growing up not knowing how I would survive when I could not even understand what was going on around me. But onward we move; time does not stop to let us figure out what is wrong with us, or to go back and undo damage, it just moves on. Inevitably, I would become a teenager and add the typical problems experienced by teenagers on top of all of those problems I already had.

INSIGHTS AND INTERVENTIONS
by Larry B. Silver, M.D.

Veronica's memories of these years are remembered more than those of her preschool years; thus, this chapter is longer and in greater detail. The themes are the same, however. She showed signs of having learning, language, and motor disabilities along with ADHD. These disorders were invisible and not recognized or understood by her teachers, other professionals, or parents. Thus, at the age when she needed the most support, understanding, and help she was criticized and made to feel even more different, inadequate, and rejected. Once again, she could only reach one conclusion: "There must be something horribly wrong with me. I am what I hear about myself. I am dumb, stupid, bad, and different."

Self-esteem in children is based on three factors: unconditional love from parents, peer acceptance, and academic success. The love she received from her parents kept her going and hoping for something better someday. The academic failures and rejection by peers were devastating to her self-esteem and her self-image. Children who have low self-esteem and trouble interpreting social cues, like Veronica, are at a higher risk for abuse or assault. Much of her adult life is spent trying to undo this damage. This type of emotional damage is never fully repaired, however. Throughout life, every time one makes a mistake or perceives a negative reaction from someone, the pain and fears of childhood flare up and stare you in the face. Back comes all of the self-doubt and pain.

Children learn because they want to please people they love—their parents and teachers. It is not until adolescence or later that students begin to learn because it gives them pleasure. It is so critical during the elementary school years to have teachers who show that they like and care about their students, and that the teachers themselves act in such a way that they can be trusted and loved in return. It is this trust and love that opens the child to taking the risk of learning.

Veronica's receptive and expressive language disabilities continued to cause havoc for her. She writes throughout this section of her difficulty with understanding verbal instructions and directions. She describes her problems with word finding and with organizing her thoughts when she speaks. As she moved into learning, her language-based problems expanded into her language-based learning disabilities. These learning disabilities became painfully apparent each year of elementary school. She entered first grade not knowing the alphabet or how to count to 10. Each year she gives examples of her reading disability, organization and sequencing problems, handwriting, and written language problems. At the end of sixth grade, she still struggled with word decoding and, at best, could sight read some words.

Homework became a reality in second grade. Her parents did not understand and listened to the teachers. What else could they do when the teachers said she was capable of doing her work but that she was lazy or not trying hard enough? Not only was she intimidated in school but now she had to go home and, through homework, reveal to her parents how dumb, lazy, and bad she felt she was. By the end of elementary school, homework was a battle zone at home.

Her difficulty with distractibility and the resulting inattention to her real problems are described on every page. Not only did she have to deal with her language, learning, and motor disabilities, but she also had to struggle to stay focused and on task.

The damage of elementary school unfolds with each page. I am reminded of Mary Shelley's novel, *Frankenstein*. A scientist creates a person from parts of dead people and gives it life. The person in this novel is obviously different but wants to be accepted and loved. He tries to be proper. His appearance and behaviors confuse and frighten the townspeople, however. They taunt and tease him. Finally, he becomes so emotionally hurt and outraged that he strikes back. Then, he confirms their fears that he is a monster. They attack and kill him.

So many children with hidden disabilities are different from birth. As I mentioned in the first chapter, some of the nerves and circuits in their brains are wired differently. They look typical but they act and behave differently. All they want is to be accepted and loved. Often, all they get is teasing and criticism. Some express their anger directly and have behavioral problems in school. Early in life, Veronica began to see herself as a monster in the true sense of Mary Shelley's monster. This image haunted her in her dreams. She wanted to be accepted and loved. Yet, her anger grew. ("I was angry that people didn't see that I was lost, hurting, and in pain.") Some let their anger out. Veronica kept her anger inside and emotionally beat herself up. Increasingly, she learned to hate herself. She punished herself. She learned to injure herself to have an excuse for not doing schoolwork. Finally, the damage was done; by the age of 7, she began to feel the ultimate anger against herself: She began to consider suicide.

Her classmates and neighborhood children, possibly following the lead of her teachers, added to her rejection and pain. She gives such heart-wrenching examples of rejection and cruelty by peers. Like the *Frankenstein* monster, she only wanted to be accepted and loved. Also, like this story, she is rejected, taunted, and teased. There was no escape. Learning disabilities are lifelong disabilities. They do not restrict themselves to school. When she went to Brownies, her reading disability resulted in embarrassment and more rejection. This external feedback was internalized, and she became increasingly self-critical. Now, even she had become her own enemy. She had difficulties with relating to others and recognizing social cues. By the time she was age 7 or 8, Veronica's life was sad and overwhelming. No one understood her. Now, even she did not understand. Everyone blamed her. She even began to blame herself.

Veronica's parents loved her. They also respected her teachers and the institution of education. When teachers told them that Veronica could do her work if she tried, they believed them. When teachers told them she was "slow," they accepted this as fact. Later, when they were told she was "not bright," they accepted this. *Teachers often do not understand the status they have with parents.* A throwaway phrase used in a brief conversation can become a parent's way of thinking about his or her children for years and years. How crucial it is for teachers to be aware of this. How essential that they use no words with significant meaning without the test data to confirm their view. Educators and parents can take many positive steps to recognize and communicate concerns related to students' potential disabilities. If anyone suspects that a student may have a hidden disability, then it is important to begin collecting data that can be given to parents and other professionals.

Teachers and parents can collect student work samples that illustrate handwriting and problem-solving strategies. They can observe or video-tape the child reading aloud and interacting with peers or siblings, for example. Anecdotal data can be collected from other teachers, parents, guidance counselors, and others who know the child well. Through these and other methods, red flags may emerge that will help pinpoint the child's needs so that he or she can be referred for the appropriate testing or to professionals who can help. In addition, teachers can try different instructional strategies employing hands-on activities and other tasks that make use of learning style theories in order to reach every student.

Adolescence is that phase of development when one learns to move from being a child to becoming an adult. It is critical that the child who enters this stage of life feels successful and has a positive self-image and good feelings of self-esteem. Veronica had none of these essentials as she moved into adolescence and on to junior high school. The damage of her childhood could only lead to greater struggles as she grew into an adolescent. She ends this section of her book by hinting about how true this was for her. She accepted that how she looked was more likely to be accepted positively than how she used her brain. Use your looks and "be cute" (later, seductive) to be accepted. Don't think or use your brain and show how dumb you are. What a negative and dangerous self-belief to have on entering adolescence. She introduces us to what her adolescence will become with self-abuse and escape through substance use.

3

CHANGES AND CHALLENGES

MIDDLE SCHOOL YEARS

One night the pain
became too much. I came
completely apart in the
middle of preparing
dinner.... I began
to scream hysterically....
I could not define why;
I just came unglued.

I entered middle school, what we then called junior high, in a new school with all new students. My parents were afraid to send me to public school because I did not do well the year before, so instead I moved to a very small parochial school. I'll never forget entering that school; I was so scared, so alone. The building was small. It consisted of one small hallway, marble floors, tile walls, a 1950s decor in a parochial school setting. My mind screamed, "nowhere to hide." I didn't have my required uniform yet. How I wished I had! This became just one more way that I stood out. At this age it is so painful to feel weird—so scary to think you won't be accepted. I developed faster than a lot of the girls did, and I was embarrassed about this and the quick attention that was paid to me by the boys and the girls. My intuition told me that I was the outsider; I would have to work hard to fit in here. It wasn't going to be easy. I wanted to run back, I wanted to find the monster. Facing the monster might be easier than facing the kids. I had never met anyone like me, I didn't think there *was* anyone like me; everyone else seemed to do so well. I was completely alone.

Much to my surprise, it wasn't too long before I had many friends. At that time I wondered why both the boys and the girls liked me so much. I suppose it was because of my appearance. In my mind it couldn't have been because I was smart or nice or socially graced. At this stage of my life, I was beginning to internalize negative messages about myself. It wasn't just about school anymore; now what I thought of as my stupidity was affecting every aspect of my life—both in my mind and in reality. I couldn't figure out people's reactions to me, and my intuition told me this would be a difficult time. Now I had to deal with several conflicting issues: Was I liked for me or because I was cute and appeared to be outgoing? Is that how I found friendships? What was I doing? Was this right? Could I get by on my looks? I still hated myself; I would have rather been smart than attractive. In my adult years, I learned the answers to some of these questions I had. Unfortunately, it wasn't a pleasant truth.

Like all the other years, somehow I found a way to get through it: the overwhelming feeling of being lost, of not understanding a word that was being taught day after agonizing day as I moved from reading, to math, to social studies, to science, to religion. There had to be a way out of this torture. Fortunately for me, I found an outlet to escape the academic world, and it worked like a charm: my talent with the organ! I became the designated organist for mass every day of the week! Teachers loved me for it; students couldn't wait for me to ask them to assist me. Great! I had to practice, right?! So almost every day, I was excused from any number of classes to practice the organ in the church. It was fun; I usually tried to take my new friend, Donna. She could read music very well, so for what I lacked in reading the notes, she would read them to me. I figured out the rhythm and away we would go! I had become "the church lady" (kid) and it was not so bad at all, at least not for now. Don't get me wrong, I got nervous sitting up in the front of the church with all of my peers watching me, sneering at me, and laughing when I messed up, but it was better than reading. I was doing something none of them could do, so let them laugh! This job became mine both on weekdays for 2 years and weekends for 4 years.

Oh, the benefits of getting away. Besides, how many parochial teachers would give the dedicated church organist failing grades?! Unfortunately, there were a few. I had the pleasure of meeting one who discovered my problems and was an angel and another who had such contempt for me,

Veronica as a preteen: Happy on the surface

47

even in church, that she would glare at me with disapproving eyes. The two teachers were like night and day. The gentle teacher taught reading, the demanding teacher taught science. This reading teacher treated everyone with kindness; it flowed from her. She made such an impression on me that I concentrated on developing some of her graciousness in my adult years. Her compassion allowed me to continue to get up in the morning and come to school, to push on. She was a light in my very gloomy and uncertain world. She worked hard to help me read—phonics, memorization—you name it, we tried it all but nothing worked. At a parent–teacher conference she talked with my parents privately. "Your daughter is a sweet, very smart young lady." I think my parents had only heard this type of comment one other time, and that was when I was a very young child. The word "smart" must have been so comforting to them. "She is trying so hard to read but just doesn't seem to get it; I don't know for sure what is wrong, but I think she has a reading disability," the teacher told them. They were not surprised, but unfortunately, they still were not given any information on what could be done, where to go, or what to do. Not even the teacher knew; I know because I believe she would have told them.

The science teacher was the opposite of this wonderful woman. If there is evil in the world, to me she was certainly one source of it. Each day when I went to her class, it was a traumatic event. I wondered what would happen to me next—would I again be humiliated? What choice words would she use with me that day? One day during a science experiment, she decided to use my notebook as an example of what "not to do" when doing a project. She stood in the front of the class and opened my notebook (which was filled with letters that looked like chicken-scratches, misspelled words, confusing sentences, and the wrong hypothesis and conclusion). "You will all notice several things wrong with Veronica's work," I remember her saying. "First, she is sloppy, a sign of laziness. This will result in a one letter-grade lower. Next we have misspelled words—many of them—another sign of laziness, another letter-grade lower. Finally, a lack of ability to follow easy and specific instructions. The whole thing is wrong. The result, an F. I will not tolerate this lack of effort and lack of concern; obviously you don't care at all about your grades or your future." The tears still well up in my eyes as I recall this story. Wasn't it enough that it was such as mess?

Regardless of the news the kind teacher told my parents, I was still in a serious situation; I had to have help, and that help came from a very dear friend, the same friend who helped me read the music notes. It's very important for me to mention Donna. When I left Carolyn, my childhood friend who helped me so much, I was terrified that I would not find anyone who could possibly be like her. I was wrong. Like Carolyn, Donna was a good friend who also helped me academically. She always let me copy her homework, cheat on tests, and at the same time never made me feel like I was less of a person than she was. Donna and I were very good together; she didn't have many friends, and many of the kids treated her poorly, too. She had a very serious skin allergy; most of the kids did not understand, nor did they try. I understood her pain, and she understood mine. It was as if we knew what the other was feeling without really ever needing to express those feelings. We just simply understood one another, and we were inseparable. Donna and I would remain friends forever.

I'll never forget the first time I spent the night with Donna. She asked me lots of questions about my life, and I asked her many about hers. I learned about her fears, frustrations, and problems; she learned that I had fears of my own. "Veronica, how come you need so much help in school, I mean—you seem bright, do you just not like school?" she asked me. I was amazed at her question; I had never been asked that before. No other kids had told me that I was bright, not like that. I responded to Donna, "I don't know, I think I just don't have talent in this area. It's like for me, I understand other things, things that don't seem to matter in school."

She looked at me very curiously. "I understand that, I like school for learning, but I don't really like the kids. They make fun of me." I hugged her, knowing those words all too well. Every child should have a friend like this; everyone deserves to be cared for and accepted.

Junior high school taught me a lot about myself. I had found a team of friends, not the popular crowd by any means, but certainly the most sensitive, the smartest, and the most compassionate. I also learned that my looks were far more important to people than my brain. Of course, this hurt my self-esteem far more than anything did. But if not my looks, what else could they like? Because I didn't like myself, and because I was not successful in school, I had to get control of something.

I began to realize that my life would always be full of struggle. Up to this point it had been nothing but. I would pay the price of having a learning disability, and having learning disabilities in conjunction with all of the other problems I had would cause me to question my purpose in living. It was like an awareness that came over me; I began to realize more than ever a feeling of nothingness. I couldn't read well, in fact I knew I read so very poorly that I could not even figure out a pay phone. The pain was so great that I had to find an escape. One night the pain became too much. I came completely apart in the middle of preparing dinner. Everyone was standing around talking casually, and I began to scream hysterically. I ran out of the house clinging to the porch post crying uncontrollably. I could not define why; I just came unglued. I was coaxed back into the house and put to bed, but for weeks afterward I was overly down and lethargic. This incident was viewed as a passing thing in my house; after all, I was just a kid, and depression in children was unheard of. Of course my parents were afraid and concerned, but they assumed it was from fatigue. They were aware of the problems I was having in school, but the connection between my school problems and this episode did not happen. We had no way to define my problems; they were doing all they knew how to help me make it by keeping me busy with music, encouraging friendships, and choosing the right high school. After all, I was making average grades; it was the best we could hope for for me. They had no idea just how I was making those grades, cheating my way through, being socially promoted. They had no idea I could barely comprehend the stories in a second-grade book.

Time had come, and high school was approaching. There weren't many choices, either public or parochial. I had already spent 2 years with these kids in junior high who were going to the parochial high school, and I knew my comfort level would be higher because I had my friends. However, I had heard that the parochial schools were more difficult, that I would have to work harder. I wasn't sure how that would happen, but I couldn't risk not having my friends, not just to have someone to hang out with, but because I needed them to help me get the grades. My parents and I discussed the options, and the decision was made. I would go to the parochial school. My dad looked at me with very serious concern. "Veronica, you have promised you would try harder all throughout school; you have to do more in high school. They won't be as patient with you; it won't be as easy to slip by."

"I know, I will do it, I will try and work much harder, to do my homework whether I need to or not," I answered him. Now I had done it, I thought. I had made a commitment to my parents and to myself. Maybe they are right; maybe if I just keep working, eventually I will get it.

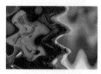

INSIGHTS AND INTERVENTIONS

by Larry B. Silver, M.D.

Middle school is a big part of that bridge from childhood to adolescence. One stage phases out and the other phases in. Veronica's parents tried to help by placing her in a smaller, private school. Many parents feel that smaller classes will help. But Veronica reminds us that smaller means that you cannot hide in the crowd. Children reject each other even more often for any differences they observe when the choice of friends is limited. Ideally, no matter what type of school a child attends, if teachers or parents have concerns, then it is best to investigate in order to establish the root causes, whether the child appears to have problems socially, academically, or both.

Most learning at the middle school level is based on the ability to read books, instructions, questions, and other materials; to be able to put your information and ideas down on a piece of paper with good vocabulary and organization as well as with the proper spelling, grammar, punctuation, and capitalization; and to be able to do math that is based on previous mastery of essential facts such as addition, subtraction, multiplication, and division. Is it any wonder that she writes about "the overwhelming feeling of being lost, of not understanding a word that was being taught day after agonizing day"? School was torture. The only escape was her music. Succeeding with music did not make up for her learning difficulties, however.

During some of her school years, Veronica had good teachers. She thrived, took the risk of learning, and enjoyed school. Then there were the other years and teachers. To me, any teacher who intimidates or embarrasses a child, such as the one described who displayed Veronica's disorganized notebook and papers to the other students and used Veronica as an example of what a lazy and bad student does, could be accused of child abuse. Teachers have an enormous impact on a child's life and can use that influence positively. If you see any signs that a student is struggling or having behavior difficulties, it is so important that you collaborate with others in your school. Perhaps a special education teacher could come to the classroom to observe the student or a guidance counselor could arrange testing. Again, it is important to collect data rather than to rely on memory or emotions related to the child. Teachers may view some children who have ADHD and related disabilities as troublemakers, but it is very possible that these students' behavior has an underlying cause.

Learning disabilities are present in every area of life. This reality has an even greater impact when one is an adolescent. If you cannot read in school, you cannot read the menu or telephone book or movie or TV guide. Life is full of failures and the need to find ways to cover them up so others do not notice. The pain Veronica associated with school, with peers, and with life led to even more self-doubt, self-criticism, and self-anger. At times, she would explode, such as the time at home when she suddenly began to scream hysterically. The "lid" came off that kept this anger and pain under control, and her feelings poured out.

As high school approached, she was still being told that the problem was with her. If only she would try harder, she could do it. No one stopped to realize that her reading skills at the end of middle school were still on the first- or second-grade level. This is a true shame. Children want to learn to read. If they are having trouble mastering reading skills, most likely there is something inhibiting them from doing so. Veronica had reading problems. She also had problems with oral instruction and attention. As she writes, school failure can be devastating to self-esteem. Veronica finally accepted what she heard from teachers and parents as she moved on to high school. She promised herself she would try harder. Only, deep inside she knew that she had been trying as hard as she could for years, and she doubted that she could try any harder.

4

DEMONS OF THE DAY

HIGH SCHOOL YEARS

I had a new monster
developing, a big one that
would replace the old
monster of ignorance.
This monster was
easier to deal with, the
monster of my bodily
image.

Some students look forward to high school. Others can take it or leave it. And still others, such as me, dreaded going, staying after, or coming back the next day. Even after I graduated from high school I would dream of not having graduated and having to do it all over again—a thought that still haunts me today, even though I have earned a master's degree.

High school was a nightmare, at least in the academic sense. The severity of the pain associated with the academic problems began to cause havoc on other aspects of my life as well. I was learning that to be independent, all those things I couldn't do very well were required. Socially, I was okay at this time in life. I had a few good friends (the same ones from eighth grade), and soon I would make even more. The boys really liked me, maybe a little too much, but that was important to me at the young age of 14. What did I know? Unfortunately, boys and other distractions consumed most of my existence in high school. This was the age at which I began to experiment with illegal substances. Most people say they get involved with substances because of peer pressure. Not me; I did it as a means of control, a means to escape from reality. No one ever pressured me to do drugs or to drink. I did it only because I hated myself.

Between the boys, alcohol, and marijuana, school was tolerable. My daily life at school was clouded, however, because of these substances and distractions and because of my own state of denial. Of course, those things masked my painful existence. It was my subconscious mind that was absorbing all of the pain those days. Because I was suppressing my feelings, I would pay an even bigger price because of this self-destructive behavior.

The first day of high school seems like yesterday. I was nervous, actually scared to death. The one blessing was that my friend Donna was there with me as well as a couple of other really bright friends. I knew they would help me just like they did in seventh and eighth grade. My parents wanted me to go to the parochial school for the same reasons they wanted me to go to the junior high. They were concerned that I would be "gobbled up" in a big school. Truth be told, that is exactly what I wanted; if I were gobbled up, no one would notice me.

It wasn't long before I would experience the torment I would endure at the hands of most of the teachers at the new school. I would be embarrassed beyond belief in high school, in a less-than-saintly religion class. Though I had been called names, stood over, and made an example of previously, this situation beat all. Daily punishment was inflicted on me for my lack of ability. Almost every day this teacher had us stand up at our desks and read out loud from the bible or a religion book. It was tough enough to read, but to stand and read, this man was simply asking too much. I could feel a cold sweat break out across my face. This man—this class—terrorized me. He hated everyone, or so it seemed, especially me. You didn't have a chance with this guy. I had to resort to other things. I used all the excuses in the book, losing my place, forgetting my homework, faking illness, forgetting my glasses, and excusing myself to go to the bathroom. Now normally, I would not use this many excuses. I didn't have to; most teachers did not require line reading everyday. He was from the old school; it didn't matter that we may not understand a word we were reading, we would have to read aloud anyway.

Recently, I saw two of my high school girlfriends when I was in town visiting my parents; one was Donna, the other was Alison, a girl I met in high school who was such a kind and bright girl. She became one of my allies as well. When I was discussing this book with them they both piped up and said, "You remember what our religion teacher used to do to you in ninth grade? Don't you remember?" asked Alison.

"Of course, some of it," I answered.

"Well, I remember one day in particular when we were all handed back a test. I got an A, and remember thinking, 'great, but the test was so easy, I didn't expect anything less.' Then, our wonderful teacher handed you your test, do you remember what he said?" I honestly did not remember. I probably blanked it out; it had happened so many times and by so many teachers that I was not shocked to hear Alison's response. Donna piped up and said, "I remember that day. I felt horrible for you."

They went on to tell me how he made me hold up my paper and tell everyone I had gotten an F. He yelled at me and told me how very stupid I must be to fail such a simple test. Alison said that I had tears in my eyes and was very upset. As they went on describing his cruelty, I began to remember it like it was yesterday. This experience was not an isolated one, in his class or in others. For the most part during my time at this school, I was either ignored or ridiculed in front of other students. It didn't matter; after one month of going from class to class and feeling inadequate, I was becoming numb. I was directing my attention to other things— mainly to the guys in school—and it wasn't difficult to get their attention.

I found it easy to attract one of the most desired upper- classmen in the school. I had a very flirtatious manner with the guys; it just seemed to come out naturally. He was so handsome and mysterious. He drove his own car, an Audi, which to all the other girls was a big deal. This attraction to this kind of thing was something I had just learned about. His family owned a very successful clothing store. I fell head over heals in (first) love with him. He was so good to me. It took some convincing, but my parents decided that because he was so nice, I could start car dating. I think in some ways they felt sorry for me because I was having trouble in school. It was a way to fit in.

We spent as much time as we could together, more time than my parents knew about. Often I would ride my bike to school, 10 miles each way; this allowed me to get there earlier. Then as the weather changed, I would carpool with my mom and Donna's mother, who was her friend, who would drop Donna and me off early. My boyfriend and I had lots of time to see each other. Oh, how the rumors would fly about the two of us and most were not true. Unfortunately, the one thing I did get into that was harmful was substances. My boyfriend had all the resources that went along with being popular and an upperclassman. Though I knew intellectually that this was dangerous, I wanted desperately for him to like me and for me to fit in with his friends. For a girl who wanted an escape, this was a match made in heaven. I learned very early that using these drugs produced a very comforting effect, and I could fool just about everyone that I wasn't under the influence of anything, everyone that is, except the kids. They knew exactly what I was doing, the same thing many of us did. For me, the rationale was that it was better to be stoned or drunk than slow and stupid.

The partying started out innocently enough but became routine for us; we would either drink a little Southern Comfort or smoke a little pot before school. I could buzz for hours on this stuff. Earlier I talked about how much I hated my religion class; after I started using drugs and alcohol, it just didn't matter as much. I used to frustrate this teacher to no end. I simply did not react to his cruel intentions anymore. As a matter of fact, I ignored him. In my mind, I had become invisible. Ironically, he never sent me out of class; he either didn't care what I was doing or he couldn't figure out what was wrong with me. So my maladaptive behaviors as well as my learning problems were being ignored.

During the time I was dating my first high school boyfriend, I had all kinds of fun. It wasn't just the drinking and smoking pot. It wasn't just going to sports events and seeing how straight we could act. It was the fact that he, a popular upperclassman, accepted me and cared about me, at least as much as a teenage boy can care. He never pressured me into sex or into doing anything that I didn't want to; he was very respectful. Unfortunately, as with most relationships in the teen years, things started going the wrong way. And actually it was me who pushed the relationship into failure. I had this ability to talk him into doing anything, and one day I got him into very big trouble. I remember sitting in his car; we had no drugs or alcohol (a good thing). I told him I wanted to drive his car. He looked at me and said that I couldn't, but I used my innocent charm and the next thing I knew we were on our way. It was a crazy idea; driving close by the school in a small town whizzing past everyone, not caring about a thing. I had no driver's license—not even a learner's permit.

We had a blast. Our good time came to an end once we got to school, though. Somehow during our fun ride, the principal of the school spied us. Later that morning, we were both pulled into his office and did we *ever* have fear drummed into us. I was told how very stupid this was, and that I had placed myself, my boyfriend, and his family in jeopardy. The fear in my face and my uncontrollable tears must have softened him. He chose not to call my parents. The same fate did not befall my boyfriend, however. His parents were called, and he told me the next day that he was not allowed to see me anymore, but he didn't care—he wouldn't listen to them.

We tried to sustain the relationship in secret but the pressure was too much for him at home and he caved in, which was not unexpected from a guy his age. At my age, however, I couldn't see that. When all of this occurred, I was depressed beyond belief. Fortunately, at that time I made a new friend; her name was Joanne. She was just what I needed during my time of desperation. She was wild, funny, and very intelligent. She helped me get through my classes, but she also joined in with me on my destructive behaviors.

I remember the nights we would go to the park: We'd laugh for hours; I could think more clearly, probably because I was more relaxed. I could see things somehow differently; in my mind it wasn't the drugs that caused this, but an unsuppressed intelligence that I could not feel when I was in school. That wandering, drifting mind I had always had, those quick-processing skills, those millions of ideas, all became more manageable. I began to find that without those drugs I just wasn't the same. I liked myself when I was funny, quick, and out of touch with reality. It didn't hurt as much. I only learned as an adult that I was probably self-medicating my ADHD and what was an emerging mood disorder. But mostly, I believe I was suppressing my insecurity.

By the end of my freshman year, I had developed quite a reputation: the party girl, always a lot of fun. Unfortunately for me, I also developed a reputation regarding how I was with boys, which wasn't accurate. One event that led me into dangerous waters was a party I attended. All I wanted to do was to have fun, to fit in. It was at that party that I would learn more about a guy who would be in and out of my life for many years to come.

I had been invited to this party by my best male friend's older brother, so he and I decided that because they were juniors and we were freshman, we would be big-shots and bring our own alcohol. It only took one glance to see that I was the only girl at the party. With no chance of keeping pace with the others, we began a race to see who could drink the two pints of Southern Comfort the fastest (a practice known as "shotgunning"). I knew deep down the risks I was taking—both by being the only girl there and also by drinking enough to kill a person. But for me at that time, I just wanted to fit in. I wanted to be the same, to not feel different, ignorant, unattractive, and to temporarily remove my self-doubt.

Of course, instead of fitting in, I almost became a victim of a vicious crime; a few boys dragged me off with the intent to assault me. That was when Kyle came along, a guy who had been following me for months, wanting to date me, though I hadn't been interested. I thought he was strange. But because it was him who stopped the guys, I felt that I owed him. He took me home that night in his mom's car, a Mercedes Benz. Of course I got sick but he didn't seem to mind. He took care of me and helped me walk as much of it off as I could.

When we arrived at my house I could walk well enough to get inside. My parents stopped me in my tracks and said, "You've been drinking." I admitted it, how could I deny it? I knew I smelled awful, my clothes were a mess; I was a mess. I told them I had had two beers but certainly not "the hard stuff." Fortunately, or maybe unfortunately, they believed me. Still, I was grounded for a month—and I deserved it. My parents did what any parents would do and they were right to do it, but unfortunately they did not inquire as to why their 15-year-old daughter came home in such a state. They were just rightfully angry that I was such a mess. I know now from having talked to them that had they had more education on teen behavior, drinking, and drugs they would have sent me to counseling. Again, I was a victim of a time in which people lacked information about my types of disabilities, which led to many more damaging events in my life.

After that time, I began to see Kyle differently, and we began dating. He was special in some ways; he saw into me somehow, perhaps because he had his own pain. He, too, was different. Lots of kids teased him; they didn't treat him very nicely. He wasn't all that attractive, but he understood me and he gave me a lot of attention. He convinced me that I needed someone to take care of me. Perhaps he was right; after all, nothing had gone right up to this point.

I would soon come to see Kyle as a master of manipulation; he used the right words and did the right things. I'll never forget that first night when we were in my parents' back yard and he told me how the kids at school thought I was a "whore." I couldn't understand that because I had not even been with anyone. He told me the other kids didn't like me. He knew exactly how I would latch on to his information. It hurt to think that my flirtatiousness, my drinking, my drug use, and my hyperactive behavior got me into this much trouble. But if that was the impression people had of me, it had to stop. I had to make a change. So we made a deal: I'd be his girl-friend and he would protect me and provide me with my favorite drinks under his supervision. He would be with me all the time; no one would ever hurt me. It was like offering the world to me at that time in my life and at the same time removing a part of my life a little bit at a time. What I didn't realize was that for all this comfort and protection, both from other men and from the pains of being at school—I was losing a little of myself by allowing him to take over for me. If you are insecure and afraid it's easy to give in to a relationship that is controlling; after all, control was what I lacked, so maybe he could change me. It was likely that even if I had seen the negative aspects (which I did, in some way), I would not have changed my relationship with him. After all, he liked me for who I was, full of flaws, dumb, and without much hope of a positive future—at least in my mind. So he became "my protector" who shielded me from many painful problems, my past, and my feelings of ignorance. He needed to have control and I needed to be controlled: a deadly match that at first appeared heaven sent.

Over time, Kyle and I became very close, always spending time together. He told me what to do, where to go, how to act, and what to wear. I no longer had to worry about making mistakes—he would protect me. I did not realize at that young age just how very destructive this relationship was for both of us. It didn't matter, because at 15 going on 16, I, just like most kids my age, "knew it all." We were an item at school, respected by other students. Like a married couple, we went everywhere together; it was as if we *were* a married couple.

Soon into this relationship, I had developed this distaste for marijuana and begged Kyle to stop his own use. This was in some ways ironic, but after watching other people smoking pot I saw it as so unattractive and so stupid, it just turned me off. As a matter of fact, I began to see many things in life as stupid: other people, what they did, who they talked to, what they wore. It was a kind of self-protection: "If everyone is stupid, then I guess it is not so bad for me." Of course, I could not become too grandiose. I continued to drink, as did he.

The problems at school continued to worsen. The classes became much more difficult. My sophomore year was very troublesome, but I did have something to look forward to—my driver's license. I would be free to explore my world, listen to my music, and drive as fast as I wanted to. I wasn't afraid of much. I took many risks during this time, including with my own life. I was too immature to realize, at that time, that other lives could have been ruined.

I bought a little Volkswagen Bug before I was 16, and luckily for me my mom would drive it occasionally to her friend's house, leave it there, and carpool with her. The fact that my car was left somewhere where my parents couldn't see it gave me the perfect opportunity after school to sneak it away for a spin. It was really crazy that I would take this type of risk. Anyone could have seen me. One of the adults at the house where it was supposed to be parked was a highway patrolman. To this day, as many times as we went out, I can't believe I wasn't caught. I remember several occasions in which I was nearly involved in a collision. These potential wrecks were not due to my inability or lack of experience with driving, but because I drove very fast. It was as if I was begging to be caught, to be hurt, or to die. Someone had to help me. Maybe if I screwed up royally, then someone would ask why I was engaged in such reckless behavior.

For me, having control in my life was what I needed, and driving was one way I got that control. I used to love to drive. It was a release. I had lightning-fast reactions: I could get in and out of almost anything in a driving situation and I felt freedom as I never had before. I was in complete control—or so I thought. It would have been devastating if I had not passed my driving test, and actually I did not pass it the first time. But I was determined. Once more I hid the fact that I was having trouble reading and under-standing written directions. I memorized that driver's manual. I had my friend read it to me as I read along, memorizing the words. I had my parents quiz me over and over. I was determined to learn it. Once I passed, I was free. It was a great feeling. What I didn't realize then was that having that multisensory input was what it took for me to succeed and would be my key to learning success in the future. I couldn't read or comprehend very well, but I could memorize well enough to pass a basic test.

Fortunately for me, my parents put a condition on my having a car. I would pay for it and the insurance. This was a very positive lesson for a young person, to learn a little about the real world by learning that money doesn't grow on trees. This meant I had to get a better job; up to this point, I had been babysitting. So, exactly one month past my 16th birthday, I went to a movie theater, one in which a friend worked, and I was hired on the spot. Getting the job was too easy; of course I had the application in advance, and Kyle helped me fill it out. But it was the interview that surprised me; I discovered I had a little "gift." I could talk my way into just about anything. I had turned into a major flirt and an interesting conversationalist when I would turn on the charm, at least for a teenager. I had watched and observed so many people over the years that I was able to act out the appropriate parts at the right times. All that studying had paid off!

The job was perfect for me. One of the perks was that on most days of the week I could go to the movies free with a friend. I was a major movie and television nut. I wasn't allowed a lot of these things until I was in my teen years, but the movement, the action, and the changes in sound and color mesmerized me. It was all quite stimulating. When I watched movies and television, my brain would shut off. I can't really remember it shutting off in any other instances—except, of course, when I used substances. Shutting off my mind was a good thing because it was always running, linking to a multitude of things. Usually my mind reminded me of what a computer does when you type in a directory and it runs over everything you have in there very quickly; you can't make sense of it. My mind ran so fast that sometimes it would wear me out. I could never have just one thought going through my mind at one time. For me it had to be many thoughts, and sometimes they were uncontrollable.

My job at the theater was to work the concession stand. It couldn't be that hard. The prices of the items for sale were all similar, and the tax was already built into the cost of each item. I knew I was terrible at math so I made a little cheat sheet (even at that age I knew how to be self-accommodating) with all of the possible costs and the change I would have to give back. Every once in a while someone would give me a $50 bill. It would stump me terribly. I couldn't figure out how to give the change back. I remember being so embarrassed. Customers would get impatient and laugh at me. I wanted to climb over the counter, all 100 pounds of me, and smack them as hard as I could. Eventually I would have to depend on the customers to tell me how much to give them. Fortunately for me, most people were honest, but unfortunately I felt that all eyes were on the "idiot." Although I may have felt this way, I also began to develop coping skills for my lack of ability. My intuition, coupled with my interpersonal skills, allowed me to find a way to get answers and help from many people. In later years, I would learn to hone these skills even more. I would also learn later that these skills would be misinterpreted—and with potentially devastating results.

The rest of my tenth-grade year brought more opportunities for the development of my self-doubt, not because I struggled more; it was the same as years before. But getting help and passing classes became more challenging; Donna couldn't be in every class. I knew it was hopeless. I didn't even want to see my future sometimes. I couldn't even remember the simplest of instructions given to complete an assignment. So as the classes became increasingly difficult, teachers and counselors would begin to notice more.

That spring I was asked to go to the counselor's office. It was there that reality hit hard. Her words were powerful. "Veronica, your grades would indicate that you are not going to graduate with your class if you don't shape up. You have to put more time into your studies. Next year, the coursework will get more difficult, and you will have to work even harder. You know that in your math class you are not doing very well; as a matter of fact, you are close to failing. You have already received one F in Art History.

You are going to have to try harder, buckle down. Are you willing to do that?" Never did she ask me if I knew how to study, or if I could even read or understand what was being taught, she just used the catch-all words, "try harder," or I would not graduate.

In my mind I was feeling that I was lazy and slow—an unmotivated kid—even though she personally did not use those words. When I would think of myself this way, I would perseverate on them to the point where I would spend hours of time and energy covering up my failures. One way I would do this is to work as many hours a week as I could at my job. There, I found peace and fulfillment; I was good at something. I knew I could run circles around the other employees, fixing things, working faster at cleanup than anyone else, always looking for more to do when it was slow. So was I really slow? Was I really lazy, when my mind would race to come up with new ways of doing odd jobs? Was I really unmotivated? Not in my job; there I was happy. Despite the pain and failure I experienced in school, I still got up each day and faced it head on. I would find a way, somehow.

Unfortunately, the tug of insecurity began to create more devastating emotional struggles. I began to develop more behaviors to control my environment, or so I thought I could control it. Denial became my companion. I could drink to create comfort in my head. I could cheat and believe in a strange way that I had actually done the work myself. I cheated so convincingly the teachers never doubted me. I could laugh about my grades, receiving each D and F as if it were no big deal. I'd been getting them so long that it began to seem normal. By now it didn't matter. I didn't care anymore, or so I convinced myself. I would somehow get by on my looks, love of people, insight, hard work, and musical ability. It didn't matter how, I just would. Deep down I hated myself; I just wasn't ready to admit it. Instead, I acted out. I learned self-destructive behaviors, stayed in an addictive relationship in which I became controlled, and tried to convince myself I was something different than I was. All along I knew exactly who I was—a failure, I was just hiding behind a facade of success that had become so real that even I sometimes believed it.

Somehow I was able to get through the rest of my tenth-grade year. At one point, I was asked to work an hour per day as an assistant to a second-grade teacher. Okay, it was an opportunity to get out of a difficult class, but I didn't know until I entered the room that first day just how much I would be challenged even here. It was the work the teacher wanted me to do—to read to the kids, grade papers, and help them with their homework. I found I was inept, even with subject matter targeted toward much younger children. I could read some of the stories but I would stumble over some words. The task that gave me the most difficulty was grading math, English, and other papers. I could not do it without a teacher's answer sheet, and many times because the work was so simple there was not one available. I remember one second-grade boy telling me I was showing another student how to do their work the wrong way. I could feel the heat in my face from embarrassment. Soon, I was asked to not return; my help was not needed. I was never told why, but I knew the answer.

To this day, I still wonder just exactly how I even got by in the tenth grade. I received no help from my teachers, and even in study hall with someone specifically there to help, nothing was done. I asked the aide to help me a couple of times, and she would just look at me with evil eyes and tell me I was not trying enough. The only way I did succeed (if you can call it that) was to make use of my exceptional skill at cheating. After these many years of practice, it was no surprise that I was able once again to pull it off.

Once the summer arrived, I was able to take my mind off of school and to focus on having fun and working. My friends relied on me to plan activities, and I was always able to come up with something to do. Sometimes we'd go camping; other times we'd go down to the lake for the day to swim around the dock. One time we drove an hour away to spend the night in a hotel. I went to the liquor store, stocked up on the hard stuff, and went back to the room in which all of us would get loaded. Thank goodness we had the sense not to drive around drunk.

Most of my friends were neither the "popular kids" nor the "druggies." We were all kind of oddballs, looking for a place to belong. It was like a little secret brigade; the other kids thought I was weird because I had friends from all of the groups, but my favorite friends were in this group, the ones who cherished my ingenuity, my ability to find the fun for them and for me. So here I was, this hyperactive, wild, manic kid who knew how to find the fun, no matter what the risk. They simply followed along. Little did they know I was acting, and little did I know that I was in a self-destructive mode, playing with fire.

When school started my junior year, I assured my parents I would do better. It was strange, though; I felt they didn't believe me. I guess after years of promising them I would try harder, why should they believe this time would be any different? I was determined, and I was under the illusion that I could do it; I knew I must somehow be smart enough; I just had to be; my future depended on it. I would play out in my mind what it would be like to start school and all of a sudden start succeeding. I could see how surprised all of my friends and my teachers would be and how thrilled my parents would feel. I was so excited about my fantasy; I could visualize it in my mind. My daydreams would take me away; I didn't think about all the other times I had tried and failed. That was different, that was then, and this was now. I was older and more mature. "I can do this; it can't be that hard. I'll figure it out. I want this dream to be a reality. I want to be smart!" I'd tell myself.

So try I did for the first month or so, with agonizing effort. New start, new books, new classes: It was all a new beginning. I began with an open attitude, I was willing to try more than ever before. I fought my thoughts of feeling stupid; I kept pushing them back time and time again. But it was hot in the rooms, and I was distracted by the noise of the fans and the rustle of the wind through the windows. It was too much for me to sustain my focus long enough to understand any of the instruction. That was okay, I thought; I could get the information from my books; I would just write down what was on the board. I could do that. It was easy, wasn't it? Other kids could do it; perhaps through some miraculous change over the summer I could now take notes. My handwriting was so difficult to read, even for me. My reading skills were so weak; I couldn't even understand some of the words I was copying from the board onto my paper. My hand and wrist would ache from trying to copy it neatly, and before I could get it down, the teacher would erase the board. I would get the numbers and the information all mixed up. I tried to keep up, but things kept getting confused. I would hear everything; unfortunately hearing *everything* was the problem. I would get so angry trying to hear the teacher. People would cough, drop their pencils, and rattle their papers. I wanted to scream from the pressure of trying to hear her and make sense of her instruction but I had to understand. I just had to do better.

I remember taking my books home, placing them neatly on my desk, and arranging my notebooks and pens in a ready-to-use position. I had even set up my desk for study. It was clear of everything except a lamp and a dictionary. This part was easy for me; I was very organized, and my room was never out of order. I looked at the neatly organized books and the tools and all of a sudden it didn't matter that I couldn't use the dictionary well or understand the definitions. All those years of failure prior to this were my fault; I had been too busy with other things (I temporarily forgot about how hard I had tried in the previous years). The books called out to me, "I am power, I possess what you need. Read me— you will learn to understand." I remember staring at those books on the table trying to figure out how I could study. Where do I start? What do I do?

Then, as quickly as the confidence began, it ended. I was so angry with myself. Where had the years gone, I asked myself. All those people were right—I just wasted the years away! Now I was lost. I couldn't even understand what I was reading; I couldn't remember any of what the teachers had taught us. I wanted it to end. I would run away in my mind to a place that was safe, my own world in which I was the winner, in which I was recognized for what I could do. NO MORE BOOKS! With the tears streaming down my face, I would still pretend to read, but I knew the truth; I knew it was useless. I'd give up, go find a television, watch cartoons, and pretend I was still a young child. I had my whole life in front of me, and with that in mind and the television going, I could temporarily forget the pain.

I don't know why I thought I could do any better. Every day of my life I experienced mass confusion. So much information was coming in and I had so little ability to sort it out. There is a concept in education called multisensory learning. For someone with the types of learning disabilities I had it was critical that when presented with the written word, it would either be read to me or explained to me in general terms. When words were written and then spoken it made more sense, as long as these communication methods were presented together; it was when new words were written and not spoken that I would become confused. I would try to backtrack to make sense of the new word I had seen written, but I couldn't find the meaning in my mind. It was as if I had had a revelation: "Ah yes, I know that word," but I couldn't tell myself or anyone else how I knew it, what it meant, or how to use and apply it. I couldn't even remember it. "What did they say in class? Why can't I remember anything?" Then, before I knew it, I was lost—I had failed again. There's nothing worse than failing every day: My body would shake, my stomach would ache, my head would pound with pain, and I would cast my eyes down in an attempt to hide the tears. I would put on a smile, pretend to understand, and work hard at pleasing the teachers, but the grades didn't lie. Instead of improving, even when I was really trying, I did worse. I had broken a promise to myself; to the counselor; and most importantly, to my parents. I was a failure; I was worthless. A voice inside would ask, "Why do I keep pretending that I will do any better than before? Why do I keep trying all the time?" Then I'd say back to that voice, "No one cares about the fact that you are trying; it's all in the grades."

By the end of the first semester, I had made a decision, one I had to make. So had my boyfriend Kyle, interestingly enough. We both decided separately that we wanted to go to public school. This meant not only a loss of my friends who helped me through so much but also my boyfriend. He was going to a different school than I was. I had become so dependent on him to help me survive my problems, the ones he told me about and the ones I knew about. I had learned to turn to him on every issue. I told him everything, and I felt he was the only one who understood me. At least, that is what he told me, and I believed him. He had tremendous control over me. I was allowed to have certain girl-friends as long as he approved, and he told me how to dress, how to act, and where to go. I had developed an extremely unhealthy dependence on him because I felt inadequate in all other areas in life. Now what would I do with no one to protect me from myself and from school?

My mind was spinning—my thoughts were going faster and faster. I thought not only of my fear in going to that new school but about losing him to another girl, a smart girl, a girl much prettier than I was. I was terrified; it was horrible. How could I compete? My life was falling apart, but I couldn't let anyone know. I had to pretend to be happy about this change; I couldn't let anyone down; this was my only way to graduate and I had to do it. So after the first semester, I changed to the new school.

This school was much bigger than my old one. I figured the good news was that I could hide more easily. I was always looking for a positive in the negative. When signing up for classes at my new school, I learned that the requirements were different; actually I had too many credit hours and would be eligible to graduate a semester early! Oh, the thrill I had; it was overwhelming. I couldn't wait to tell my parents. Of course, there was a hitch; my counselor told me that if I were to graduate a semester early, I had to go to college. I agreed; I could do that, college was different, probably easier. No one had talked to me about college, what to expect, how to survive. But in my mind, it was simple; I would only have to go 3 mornings or afternoons a week so there would be lots of time to learn.

I went ahead and planned the second semester of my junior year and the first semester of my senior year. The classes I had to take were wonderful. I thought that I was going to like this school. It turned out that not only did I have enough credits but also many I possessed were in the courses I would have certainly failed at this new school: subjects such as math, science, history, foreign language, composition, and of course, geography. All of these classes would have been death to me. As it turned out, however, the only history class I was required to take was all discussion. Also, the only English class I had to take was one in which I would find a teacher who, for the first time in all of my high school years, would give me a gift that I wouldn't forget for a lifetime.

Because I really didn't know anyone (or so I thought), it was ideal—I didn't have to worry as much about finding a fellow student to help me get by. I signed up for woodworking, chorus, typing, physical education, and a history class. These classes were great for me; at last I had found a way to get by in school without having to cheat so much. I was concerned about the history class but it was based mostly on projects and discussion. I was good at this. The other classes I excelled in, even though I was required to do tasks such as measuring the wood needed to build things. Again, I had found that I could accomplish much by using others to help me, including getting a little help from the boys (I was the only girl taking the woodworking class). It was a breeze; they were all willing to help. What helped even more in the woodworking class was that I actually had some talent in this area, which was a big surprise to me.

It was in this school that I began to develop another controlling habit: an obsession with my weight. Ironically, I got into this through a friend at the new high school who I had actually known years before, Alison, the girl from my ninth-grade religion class. She had transferred in her tenth-grade year. Instantly we renewed our friendship. Though we did not have any classes together, we did have lunch, and together we decided to begin to diet. This worked out well for me for several reasons; one, I had a friend at lunchtime, and for me, lunchtime was very frightening because I had trouble figuring out how much things cost quickly enough to calculate if I had enough money. I would get embarrassed holding up the lines so I would choose the easy way out, which was to eat just a little and not worry about it. Second, watching my weight gave me a sense of accomplishment: I knew I could do this; I had already done it often, just not daily.

Alison, like me, saw herself as fat, though neither of us was. Even though I was 5' 5" tall and weighed 105 pounds, all I could see was that I was "chunky." Of course, now I know exactly why. It was my need to have control, and that was all that mattered. The thinner I got, the more energy and enthusiasm I developed. I could get by on an apple, rice, water, diet soda, and milk every day. Sometimes I would eat popcorn at work, a little at a time. I went from 105 to 100 to 98 pounds, finally weighing in at a meager 95 pounds. I felt euphoric; I felt that I had accomplished more than anyone else. When I walked around with a 22" waist, I believed that I had achieved what all the other girls only dreamed of being: I was model thin. I had won. But it still wasn't enough.

My problems in school concerned me less and less because I was taking classes that emphasized my strengths or that were simply easy. The fact that I felt dumb and my inability to understand the written word became almost nonissues. My obsessive focus on my looks and weight took precedence. People wonder why girls and even some boys do this to themselves. It is really quite simple—because we can, and because we want to. If you don't like yourself, you want to do something about it; if you feel out of control, you find something that you can control. The only choice left is to call it quits. I would continue to control what I thought I could despite the fact that I was endangering my health and potentially my life.

It was at this time in my life that things began to change drastically. I was becoming an adult; I would be facing the world on my own. I had a new monster developing, a big one that would replace the old monster of ignorance. This monster was easier to deal with, the monster of my bodily image. I could control her; the old monster of ignorance had already won.

It was almost the end of my junior year. A lot had occurred; Kyle had decided he wanted to go off to college in another state. I knew I would lose him there for certain, and I did. The one person who saved me (I thought) was leaving me; he wanted to date other girls. I could see him meeting those beach beauties. I could see why; after all, I was a loser. I hated him for breaking up with me. He told me we would be together forever, and I had given myself to him my sophomore year believing him. I remember thinking, "If I looked better, if I was smart, this wouldn't be happening to me." For days I would be depressed. At that time, though, all I could believe was that he had lied. He wanted to experience the world because he was bored with me. Because I was dumb and fat (or so I thought), he had good reason to be bored. What I really hated wasn't him but me; had I liked myself, I would not have even allowed him to control my emotions the way he did. How I hated myself! I just wanted it all to end.

Somehow I managed to go on, though I craved his attention and his control. I did what many people who are unhappy with their lives do; they try to buy their happiness. So I bought a new car. Then I planned a camping trip with my friends; went to many wild parties; and gained more control of my eating habits, figuring out ways to eat more and still be as thin as I liked. I still continued to drink but not as much; after all, drinking made you fat. I would only drink now on the weekends. But when I drank, I couldn't eat as much, so I developed the ability to refrain from eating more than one small meal on the weekends. I got so good at this; I would actually convince myself I could get full just smelling food. It is pretty scary, the power I thought I possessed. I did not know the extent of the destruction I was causing myself both mentally and physically.

Not only had I learned that I could control my physical self but also I learned more and more about how I was able to get things I needed based on my looks and personality. I had met a new boyfriend, Juan, who would change much of my life. He gave me healthy encouragement, support, and friendship, which I thought I had with Kyle. I was quickly learning, however, that I hadn't really experienced a healthy relationship before. I learned from Juan how a woman should be treated. And I learned what I thought was the reality of high school. It was supposed to be the primary facet of a teen's life; it was supposed to prepare you for a future. It was supposed to be the transition into adulthood. For me, it just reinforced that if adulthood is anything like high school, why try? So I learned that there was more to life than school and that my personality was one that Juan and his friends really loved. They were older (college guys) and cultured.

This new boyfriend came along at the perfect time. He was a get-even boyfriend, meaning that I was able to get back at the one guy I thought I would be with forever; a guy who took away my security when he told me he wanted to date other girls. I was entering my senior year in high school, and Juan was a junior in college. My parents loved him! He was very smooth, very attractive, very smart, and extremely well rounded. He was so good with them. They let me do things with him they never allowed with other boyfriends. I was allowed to stay out much later; he could come over even when they weren't home, and one day they let him take me to an amusement park—a 3-hour drive away! But was he ever a Romeo! All he had to do was snap his fingers and I'd be there. He showered me with gifts, love, and affection. He didn't criticize the way I dressed or what I looked like or what I said; he loved me. After 3 months of dating, he asked me to marry him. My parents were thrilled. It was during this time that we had learned something else about him; he was a multimillionaire, an heir to a family fortune.

Of course, my parents really liked him and would have liked to see me marry him one day. Although I admired him and respected him, however, there was a problem: I didn't really love him, and I was not really "in love with him." He was *too* nice, and I believed that I didn't deserve someone this nice. What did I have to offer him, anyway? I found I was still addicted to my former relationship. Kyle treated me wonderfully half of the time, and the other half of the time he treated me worse than horrible. But I thought I deserved that. After all, in my mind I was stupid, fat, and ugly. I had to decide what to do, and I had to face my last semester in high school. I would figure it out; things would happen that would tell me what to do. My mom had always told me to "look for the signs." I know now that I created the signs. I set up things to fail; I wasn't deserving of happiness. And for my mind to work well, like so many people with ADHD, I had to find a way to stimulate it, and the best way I could find at the time was with negative stimuli.

I stayed with Juan for the first semester of my senior year of high school; Kyle was still out of state. My senior year was crazy, the coursework was easy just like it was in the previous year, but I did have one class that was required and I dreaded it—English. We had to do sentence structuring, writing, spelling, all of the things I really had trouble with. The teacher was tough, but she really cared. I did try, no one could say I was a person who would give a mediocre effort—at least in the beginning stages of a class. I always started off with a new view of how things would be different.

Like so many individuals with LD and ADHD my ambition was there, but after seeing more failure, getting frustrated, and feeling confused, classes only served as a reminder not to try; it hurt too much. If a teacher was perceptive enough, however, he or she would see the struggle and really jump in to help me before my motivation would be lost. This English teacher worked with me often, after school, before class, whenever she had a moment. She didn't need to, there was really no reason for her to help me, but she wanted to help me. I think she realized I wanted to graduate this semester, and she knew if I wasn't even able to find a noun and a verb in a simple sentence that I could not pass her class. She knew I couldn't read well, and she had seen enough samples of my writing to tell her I had just slid by all these years.

I cared for her because she really believed in me, and I gave it my all. Still, nothing seemed to work. One day I'd understand it— the next day it was as if I had never learned a thing. It was so frustrating to me. I would cry in my car going home or to work with the music blaring as loud as possible hoping that it would drown the pain I had inside. Even today, I have that pain. It's a loss; it's what people probably want more than anything in life, to have the ability to fit in, to succeed. It was all a lie. Sadness consumed me much of this year as I was ending a part of my life in which I had failed; no one could undo the damage that was already done. I knew that my life would be tough; I knew then that my life was not bright. In fact, it felt hopeless.

The end of the semester when I was to graduate, I was passing all of my other classes except for English. I don't think I ever cried in front of a teacher like I did with my English teacher when I got that last test back again with an F. That day, I couldn't laugh it off anymore. But she looked at me with sadness and the kindest eyes I'd remember for many years as she spoke these words from heaven, "You passed, you passed with effort." She explained, "Veronica, you have worked so hard, I know you have, but some-how, somewhere along the line you have been missed. For whatever reason, other teachers didn't see it; they didn't know; it was as if you got by unnoticed, although I don't know how. It's not fair being where you are now. I can see your pain and have seen your effort."

With that she gave me a D, which was like an A to me. I wanted to hug her; she never knew how much that meant to me.

Looking back now, I know she gave me that D because she knew it was too late to go back. Had I failed that day, I don't know if I would be here today. Suicide ideation was and had been a part of my life for so long already. She made me promise her that I would have someone do some testing with me for a learning disability. I promised her I would, knowing full well that my intentions were to run away from the inevitable diagnosis of stupidity. To me, at that time in my life, a learning disability meant I would be classified as "retarded." So said society—I didn't know any better.

In our society we talk about the negatives of social promotion. Some may say I was socially promoted in this class; perhaps to some degree the term fits. But honestly, wasn't it the hard work that motivated her to give me the passing grade? What good would it have done to hold me back after all that effort, especially this late in the game? Isn't hard work and dedication something employers look for in an employee? I was able to demonstrate those qualities, and with the right type of encouragement and help, because of her, I did remember, and I would find an answer. She was a piece of the puzzle that allowed me to succeed and not fail. I believe she did the right thing. Otherwise, I may have wound up arriving somewhere else than I have today.

Other things changed in my life before I was to start college. Juan went home for Christmas. He was going to tell his parents he had found the girl he wanted to marry. He would be back in 3 weeks. But someone else was also coming back in town and had been calling—Kyle. He was coming back to attend college with me, and he wanted to work things out. I was confused as to what to do. My parents were outraged with me. They loved Juan; they did not like Kyle. They knew that he was controlling me; they knew that while I was around Juan I was getting better, or so it seemed. But their words meant nothing to me. Besides, with Kyle I was safe from a worse situation. He knew I was dumb and he didn't care. He loved me for who I was—an idiot, a loser, and a fraud. I could be me around him; even though he hurt me a lot, at least I knew what to expect, and for someone who lives in a world full of confusion and pain, that was better than risking being devastated by Juan, the one guy who showed me true, unconditional love.

I told Juan it was over. He was hurt so deeply but he didn't fight it. I wonder if he had, would I have stayed with him? Little did I know our paths would cross again, and little did I know that Kyle would grow to hate me for putting my honesty and trust in him when I told him about Juan and how close we had grown. I was so insecure with myself; I didn't know what was right or wrong in our relationship. All I knew was that I couldn't accept anything or anyone who was better than me, and I needed to be with someone who would treat me in the way I felt I deserved.

I had one more reason to get involved with Kyle; he would be attending the same university. We would take the same classes together, we would arrange our time together, and he could help me survive. This would be great; he could help me make it. The bad news that I would face is that he couldn't help me get through. He had a tough enough time himself due to his own lack of confidence. He just didn't fit into the college scene; he wanted to "get rich quick." Be that as it may, we began our classes, and together we would see each other fail in many ways. It was this college experience that would show me why I wasn't like everyone else and that I wasn't just stupid. There, I would find a name for what I was living with: learning disabilities.

INSIGHTS AND INTERVENTIONS
by Larry B. Silver, M.D.

The high school years are supposed to be fun. Friendships and social experiences build social skills and confidence. Academic successes build self-confidence and a positive self-image, preparing students for their future. This time serves as a bridge from childhood to adulthood. When this transition is successful, the individual's entry into any post high school life is easier, whether it be college, the military, work, or a relationship.

Veronica was on shaky ground both academically and emotionally as she entered high school. She did not start with excitement but with fear. Her parents thought that a smaller, more structured high school would be best. Veronica knew that she needed a larger school in which she would not be noticed and in which she could hide. There is no other way to describe her high school years than in her own words, "It was a nightmare." The price she paid emotionally took many years to undo.

Academic success was not to be. She focused on the only part of her life in which she had some positive experiences: her social life. Here, she found comfort and positive feedback. But nothing helped her with her fears and emotional pain. She turned—as many such frustrated students do—to alcohol, drugs, and unhealthy relationships. Soon, the impact of the alcohol and drugs added to her problems in school.

As with her earlier years, some teachers tried to understand and to adapt their program for her. More teachers, however, became angry with her because of her disabilities. Children with learning and other hidden disabilities are likely to exhibit a range of emotions and behaviors while struggling to master academic and social challenges. Teachers and peers may become easily frustrated with students with such disabilities when they do not understand the cause of these behavioral difficulties. These students are, consequently, at risk of poor or failing grades, lowered self-esteem, and even school dropout. Veronica faced frustration, embarrassment, and what at times could only be called emotional abuse. Imagine being forced to stand in front of your classmates and told to show them your failing test paper while the teacher called you names. As I read this section, I felt like saying, "Don't you see…she is in pain already…don't cause more…try to understand and help." But, I guess he did not see. He attacked her problems rather than trying to understand them. I wish I could say this story was a rare one, but it isn't. I hear similar stories all too often.

As her academic failures and struggles to handle any reading or written work increased, Veronica turned to her social world for positive feedback. She needed someone who would accept her as she was. As her self-esteem dropped, she began to feel that she was so dumb and bad that no one could like her. She sought and found boys who saw her as dumb and began to treat her as she was treating herself. She moved in and out of abusive relationships. Soon, she was caught in a pattern of drugs, alcohol, and negative relationships. As she said, "I learned very early that using these drugs produced a very comforting effect…It was better to be stoned or drunk than slow and stupid." It is not uncommon for people with ADHD and other learning disabilities to abuse substances. She increasingly turned to male relationships not as a mutually positive experience but as a way of being accepted, taken care of, and protected, no matter what the price.

I have no doubt that her parents loved her. Yet, I struggle to understand how they could watch her doing so poorly in school year after year and not seek answers. Any child or young adult who regularly struggles with schoolwork and homework or who suddenly seems to have taken up with a "wilder" crowd is exhibiting warning signs. If parents even have the slightest suspicion that their child is dealing with some of these issues that Veronica describes, then it is important that they talk with their children's teachers, guidance counselors, or others who might be in a position to shed some light on the reasons behind the problems.

As Veronica tells her story, she shows us time and again that learning disabilities are not just school disabilities. They are life disabilities. Her math problems affected her ability to make change on her job and to give the right change in the cafeteria. Her limited reading comprehension and written language skills forced her to cover up so many situations in which these skills were needed. As we follow her from ninth to tenth to eleventh and finally to twelfth grade, the story remains consistent. Most teachers reacted to her academic difficulties with frustration and anger. Veronica's tearful description of trying to read or to copy or to write suggests that she was trying as hard as she could. If there is one message that educators need to

Veronica as a teenager

get from this book, it is that no child or adolescent is lazy or unmotivated without a reason. It is important for educators and others who care about young people to try to find the reason rather than attack the behavior. A teacher could have sat down with Veronica and asked her to read or write or spell, for example. It would not have taken long to realize that there were serious problems to be understood and addressed.

5

JUST WANTING TO BE LOVED

COLLEGE AND YOUNG MOTHERHOOD

A bigger monster than
me had arrived, only
this monster would set
loose all the other
monsters I had hidden
away. This monster
would push me into
a shallow, lonely hole in
my mind.

I was terrified the day I registered at the university. It was a large campus with more than 10,000 students, and I felt like I was just another number. I remember praying I could register with my boyfriend Kyle, but his last name started with a C and mine started with an L. So off I went to get into the appropriate line. I'm sure all freshmen are afraid on the first official day of anything relating to college; the only difference for me was that I couldn't read well enough to fill out even the simple forms required for registration. What made matters worse was that I had not gone to orientation. No one in my family or at the high school had told me what to do. I guess they assumed that I would read about what I should do; too bad I couldn't read very well. Unfortunately, because I had not yet been diagnosed, I could not take advantage of the services provided by the university for students with disabilities. Their disability services department offers tremendous support; for example, that day I could have received assistance with registration.

Like many young people with LD and ADHD, however, even if I had been provided this service, with the frame of mind I was in, I would have assumed it was being offered because I was stupid and needed help. I probably would not have gone to orientation or disability services regardless of whether I'd known about it. Stubborn pride, fear, and uncertainty; this combination was a guarantee for failure in my case, and I would learn that if I wanted to hang onto these qualities, failure is exactly what I would get. When an individual is going to college for the first time and needs some advice on what to expect, it is important for parents, teachers, counselors, and others to hold a carefully planned discussion to allow the individual to open up with questions and concerns.

I did manage to get Kyle to look at the schedule with me prior to signing up. We circled all the classes we would take or attempt to get. I didn't have to figure it all out on my own, just copy onto the form what was circled. I sat at a table in the registration hall trying to find someone next to me or across from me to help but they all seemed so much smarter than me; I just knew they could tell I was dumb. It was as if it were written on my face. Finally, a young man noticed I was moving slowly and helped me put the right classes in the right boxes on the forms. He asked me if I needed any more help. I looked quickly to see if Kyle had seen him before I spoke, so I wouldn't get into trouble. He didn't like me talking to other boys. I could see him filling out some forms, so I carefully acknowledged this guy's offer of help. He was able to quickly finish filling out my papers, and I was up and back in line to pay. My only prayer now was, please let me get all these classes so I can be with Kyle. I got my wish; the classes we wanted were still open. Next I would have to go and purchase the books.

For a moment I was able to move into denial and think everything was going to be fine, but then the fear hit me again on the way to the bookstore. This is one example of the ups and downs in my moods: One minute I would be scared to death, the next, I would hear myself say, "It's only four classes. You can do this, you're only going to school 3 days a week. Just study the rest of the time; maybe the problem before was that you just didn't try hard enough, that's what everyone told you, maybe they were right." I certainly wished that were the case; then it would mean that I was just lazy and not dumb.

I managed to cover up how I felt so well that even Kyle never really knew how poorly I read, did math, wrote, sequenced, or functioned. But I had mastered getting help without people really knowing that I was actually overwhelmed with my world, with school, and even with the simplest things, such as finding books in a store or using a pay telephone. But as always, I found a way. All I had to do was to hang on to Kyle like a puppet would its master and let him take care of me. He marveled in that; it made him feel like a king. What he didn't know was that I hated being taken care of, I hated every aspect of it. But for a puppet to survive, it has to let its master and controller make its every move; otherwise it does not have the ability to function on its own.

Thinking back now, I remember that feeling of overwhelming anxiety as I looked around me, trying to make sense of everything. It wasn't the typical freshman anxiety; mine was caused by the fact that I couldn't read the cards in front of the books to match them with my schedule. Perhaps you know the system; the bookstore hangs identifying cards on the shelf in front of the book stacks listing the course number, the instructor, and the class. When I looked at them, however, the numbers and letters moved and changed, the names of some of the professors were too complicated to read, and I was afraid to ask for any help. I remember standing in front of a stack of books; my mind was working as if it was twisted metal with an electrical current going through it with no way to get out. I felt hot; the embarrassment made my face red. I quickly found Kyle and explained that I couldn't find the "dumb books," so he jumped in to help. This was a lot less embarrassing than asking the clerk; I would just hang onto him like a "babe" should and let him lead the way.

The first day of class began; it was very cold, although I don't know which was colder: the outdoors or me, shivering from fear. I went into the auditorium for World Geography class, and I'll never forget it: The room was like a theater, there were tons of seats, the floor was concrete, and the board was hard to read. I took a seat right next to my boyfriend. As the instructor began class, I noticed immediately that I couldn't understand him. The acoustics in the room were horrible, the fluorescent lighting was flickering, and the noise from two hundred or so students was overwhelming. It was like the circus I had experienced as a child, only here *I* was the clown. I felt like everyone was looking at me. I wanted to run out. "Keep your composure," I'd hear myself saying, "or they will think you are crazy."

I kept looking around the room even as the professor spoke. I wanted to concentrate, but it was as if something had control of me. I couldn't pull out of the daze, and in and out I would loom like I was having a bad dream from which I could not awaken. It wasn't until someone would touch me that I would move into a better temporary focus. A syllabus was passed out, and Kyle handed it to me. It was approximately five typed pages of dates on tests and chapters to be read. I remember noticing with horror how many quizzes and tests there were, and "no homework." Those two words—*tests* and *quizzes*—I had seen them so many times, but I felt sheer panic just as if I was reading the word *toxic*. This couldn't be; how was I going to pass? I have always failed tests. When I left that class, I was praying that the other classes would be better.

Unfortunately, all of the classes were virtually the same. I didn't know that I had chosen some of the most difficult freshman classes. No one told me to balance classes with something easy or fun, they just advised me to take the hard ones because I had to, to "get it over with." I was taking classes that would create concern in any new student; Psychology 101, History 101, World Geography, and college math. Failure was inevitable but I had to try; after all, I had to prove to myself that I wasn't dumb, otherwise I may as well die.

Though I knew after my first day this would be tough, I quickly rationalized that I had a lot of free time so I would go to the library and study, even though I didn't even know where to begin. It amazes me to this day that so many kids enter college with neither the academic skills nor the study and organizational skills. What is going on in the school systems? We teach people how to read, write, and do math, but we don't teach them how to apply the learning; how to study for enhanced learning, to think critically. We don't teach them how to retrieve resources, how to use resources, and how to communicate effectively. So few schools offer this kind of training. I think we are missing a vital link here with all students.

I would go to the big, three-story library where I would find a desk in the corner. I would be nice and neat; "that must be how to study," I thought to myself. Just like in high school, I would set it all up so that I could convince myself I could succeed; I would make sure I had highlighters, notebooks, pens and pencils, oh, and a calculator. I'd spend an hour on each subject every day. I could do this . . . I had plenty of time. As I began this masterful plan, I noticed that the trees outside were blowing rather wildly, that there were a lot of students sneezing, coughing. I wondered if I would get sick. I couldn't get sick, I had too much to do. Before I knew it, an hour would be gone and I would have accomplished nothing except a plan of how not to get sick. I would keep my desk clean and create a very nice diagram of a floor plan just like I drew in school as a child. I drew floor plans because they comforted me—they were so clean, so neat, so orderly—unlike my life.

Eventually, I would get to the studying, but there was a problem. I could not make out most of the words in the book; they were too big, too new, I hadn't seen many of them before. The print was small; the words would move around on the page as they always had. But that wasn't supposed to happen; I was in college now—it was supposed to be different. "Stop moving, damn it! I have to read this, just apply yourself, you're not trying, this is all in your head!" I would tell myself over and over and over again. Try harder; move to another subject; maybe math would be easier. Okay, get out the calculator, open the book, do you remember the steps? Look at your notes. So, the notes make no sense; that's my own fault; I screwed up again.

I remember many times putting my head on the desk—crying silently—hoping for a guardian angel to bless me, cure me, and give me a new brain. I wondered why—if I had such good thoughts and ideas—I couldn't do basic math, why I couldn't read or under- stand what I was reading. Why am I so dumb, why was I born, what purpose do I have in life? I should have married Juan; I'm too stupid to do anything else. I'd hear my inner voice say "Forget your dreams, you'll never amount to anything."

Things didn't get any better; they just got worse. All my classes were based on test grades, and, of course, I bombed. It was a psychology instructor who brought this to my attention in plain language: "You're failing this class, and there is no way to recover."

He asked to see my notes. Nervously I gave them to him, all the scribbled junk I called notes; the ones I had taken hidden by wrapping both of my arms around the small table of the desk so no one would see how poorly I wrote and spelled. He looked at me and asked if anyone ever suggested that I might have a learning disability. I looked at him sadly and said, "You mean that I'm stupid, yes." His response was surprising. For the first time someone explained the phrase *learning disability*. He told me that I was not stupid—that having a learning disability doesn't mean that. It means you have something going on in your head that causes you to learn very differently. He told me that I needed to get help, that there were methods that could help me.

This professor directed me to a couple of people on campus who could help me; it was a blessing and a curse I would have to live with the rest of my life. The first person seemed very pleasant. He talked to me for a while about my educational experiences. He asked me what classes I was taking. I stumbled because I actually couldn't remember them for a few minutes; Finally, with his probing, I was able to tell him most of the classes: "Psychology, history, some type of map class—and I forget the other one—oh, math." He then asked me about high school. I paused and looked at him curiously, asking what that had to do with college. My voice began to quiver, and holding back the tears I explained that I hated school; I went, but I really didn't learn anything. He looked at me with empathy; he explained that he felt that based on my handwriting and my failing grades, some testing would be in order to see if I had a learning disability. He explained after talking with me for an hour, looking in my notes, and observing my communication that I was obviously bright and very articulate. This could be a sign of a gap. Of course, there was a catch to all of this: I had to *want* the help. I looked up at him, feeling embarrassed, but I had nothing to lose; I was failing all of my classes and nothing I had tried had worked. "Yes," I replied, "please." His first request was to see if I was willing to do the testing, the second request was that I withdraw from school so my records would not reflect my failing grades. Once that was accomplished, initial testing would begin, which would eventually tell me what had been challenging me all of my life. I would finally understand why others (and even I) saw me as having something wrong with me.

That particular day was perhaps one of the most painful in my academic and emotional life. I'll never forget it; it is as if it were yesterday, a memory I cannot wash from my mind. It was so cold that day, no sunshine; the sky was gray and low almost as if I could grab it and be absorbed into it. I was standing outside; there was no wind and no one was around. I entered the administration office to withdraw from my classes. And if that wasn't bad enough, the woman who withdrew me from the classes was the mother of a "smart" friend of mine who was in my old high school. I remember her looking at me strangely and a feeling of embarrassment came flooding across me. I carefully explained that I was here to withdraw from my classes; that my advisor wanted me to do some other work and start back next fall. I remember looking at her face to read her nonverbal cues; they seemed to me to be saying "Sure, right, you're failing, I knew all about you from my daughter." It was a face of disbelief, a face that said that I was not cut out for college. She handed me the papers, and all they required was a signature from me. I was relieved that at least I would not have to face any forms.

I staggered outside the building, trying to maintain composure; I sat down on the steps of the administration building all alone and started crying hysterically. Inside my head it hurt: I saw flashbacks of all of the kids who called me stupid and slow; I saw my family so disappointed in me; I saw myself dead—lying in a casket. Maybe the pain would go away if I was dead. I thought of killing myself—I would struggle with this over and over. From one moment to the next I would think to myself, "Go ahead, do it," then the next second I would have the urge to "not give up. There has to be an answer somewhere."

I heard voices as classes were letting out. I quickly gathered my things and darted for my little Fiat X19. There I would take off the convertible roof, turn on the heat, crank the stereo full blast, and try to forget this pain, just overlook it. But even driving the Fiat that I loved so much couldn't take the pain away, so I headed for my mother's office at the high school in which she worked as a secretary for the vice principal.

As soon as I entered her office, she could tell I was hurting. I wasn't sure how she would react to all of this. I was so angry with myself, and if I had been her, I would have hated me. In my mind I kept saying what a worthless child I had been. But instead she treated me with kindness and warmth, which is what I needed desperately. It isn't uncommon for kids to have this feeling when they are hard on themselves; they expect that from others as well. Of course this makes it much more difficult to seek help when it is most needed. My mom, on the other hand, did not confirm my unrealistic fear but quickly took me into her boss's office and hugged me as she explained to me that the professor at the college had just called her because he was worried about me. Ironically, my mother worked with his wife. I was relieved; it felt so good to have her love. She could feel that I was in pain, and she had already been told what they suspected and was ready to move forward. What she didn't know was how serious this pain was for me. She could have no idea how much I wanted to die. I wanted to tell her, but at the same time, I knew I wouldn't; it was my secret, I knew she wouldn't understand, I couldn't even begin to know how to explain it. I just felt it growing inside.

After my tears had slowed down, she took me to talk with her boss, who had been my counselor at the high school from which I had graduated. I was afraid of her for some reason; perhaps because of her status or because of earlier impressions she had given me, including once when I had tried to skip school. But that day, I saw her differently than before. She shared with me that she thought she had a learning disability with math. This woman was smart, successful, and educated. I was amazed. She told me that having a learning disability is okay; many people have learning disabilities—many successful people. I would just have to learn how to work around this disability. I felt a little better. This gave me some hope, even though I knew I was much more obtuse than someone who just had a problem with math. She hugged me and told me to be strong.

Still, I was worried about all the typical things. Again I began to worry about what would happen when I got home; would my parents be upset with me for withdrawing from classes, angry that their money was lost and they would never get it back? But instead they expressed that they understood and knew something had to be done. They were relieved that maybe now we would begin to understand what was wrong with me. Soon we had the testing arranged at a nearby military base, and it was very grueling: It consisted of a total of 2 months of testing and some therapy to help undo a lot of damaged self-esteem.

I was sent to a team of people composed of an ophthalmologist, a psychologist, and a neurologist. Together they diagnosed me with severe learning disabilities. I had *dyslexia,* my reading comprehension tested at the second-grade level, and we also learned that I couldn't spell words that were at or above a third-grade level. I had *dysgraphia,* which they told me was based on my limited ability to write in cursive. I also struggled to print: My fine motor skills were affected. My handwriting looked like chicken scratch. I was also diagnosed with *dyscalculia*, a math disability, with my comprehension on approximately a third-grade level. It was a surprise to my parents but to me, I knew all along what they would find, at least in terms of lack of ability.

The day they told us the results I was asked by the neurologist to read out loud to my mom from a *Reader's Digest.* The doctor looked at me where I was sitting on an examination table. He picked up the magazine and opened it to a story, and to my surprise he handed it to me. "Read the first paragraph, Veronica." I was shocked. I looked at my mom; she looked at me. Tears welled up in my eyes; I knew she would soon learn the truth about how functionally illiterate I was. I could barely read it. I stumbled over the words, mixed up words, omitted words, and began to cry. I was angry at him for asking me to read out loud. He hadn't prepared me for this, and I was probably as surprised as my mom was. My mom began to cry. I could feel her pain, her disbelief, and her anguish. I am sure a sense of overwhelming guilt must have overcome her. Her pain for me, her fear, and her sadness over what I must also be feeling because I was not able to read at the age of 18 was overwhelming torment. I could sense what she was thinking: "What had gone wrong? How could this have been missed? This is too severe. How did she make it through school?"

In looking back on this strategy, I'd have to say how poorly the professionals involved handled it, not intentionally I am sure, but because they lacked education on human emotion. It hurt my mom immensely, and I am sure it embarrassed her. It was like rubbing her face in it: "Look at your 18-year-old daughter. How could you have missed this, you neglectful parent?" It hurt me to see my mom's pain that day; I felt that not only had I failed myself but I had also failed my parents. I wanted so badly to please them; after all, I was the clown, nothing got me down, and they never knew my immense pain before now. I had always hidden it. And further-more, that day I only learned what I *couldn't* do well. None of the doctors told my mom or me how smart I must be to have gotten this far making average grades. None of them told me that I could do better and that I had a lot to offer in the world. No comment was made to my mom about how resilient I must be and that she and my father must have had a lot to do with that. We were simply given the diagnosis, told I would need help, and as for going to college, well that would be nothing short of a small miracle.

Two positive events did come of this, however; now I knew that my difficulty with learning wasn't because I hadn't tried all these years and it wasn't because I was dumb. I was "learning disabled" (what they called someone at the time I was diagnosed). At least we had a name for it now. The other positive result of this meeting was that a psychologist who was part of the diagnostic team suggested I come to therapy once a week. I was pleased to know that my parents, though not supportive of therapy in general (many parents are not—it evokes fear that somehow they have failed, which is so opposite of the truth in my situation), would allow me to get some counseling. I had to learn how to deal with the information I had just received and how I would face the tremendous challenges that came with the knowledge of why I am the way I am.

In therapy I began to gain a better understanding of what was wrong with me, at least from a psychological viewpoint. I did get an enhanced sense of inner strength. I began to gain some weight; through his help, I began to understand that the control I needed was actually controlling me. My self-destructive behavior or starvation, abusive relationships, and substance issues were simply reinforcing the negative feelings I had about myself anyway. In other words, I was making a bad situation much worse. I contemplated breaking up with my boyfriend Kyle as I began to see the way he controlled me; of course, my parents were thrilled with that and supported the therapist even more for helping me see the dysfunction of that relationship. I learned so much about myself, about my internal anger and destructive behavior and my mood swings (though I had no firm understanding yet of the severity of this issue). Still, I was on the path to getting better. Therapy helped me to begin to see myself differently. Perhaps I had something to offer the world after all, though what it was at this stage I didn't know.... Maybe it was music; maybe I could go back to college and become a teacher. Whatever it was, all of that hinged on my getting and accepting the right kind of help. Now I had to learn to do other things to enhance my life. I had to learn how to learn, learn how to love myself. Those two things would be the hardest.

Therapy didn't last long enough, unfortunately; my parents became upset with me because I went back with Kyle shortly after breaking up with him. They blamed the therapist, but it really wasn't his fault; I was going through a lot of self-discovery; I had awakened a lot of painful memories, and Kyle was a comfort to me. I knew what to expect out of him, even if it was unhealthy. This relationship would have passed, and eventually, many years down the road it did. But when Mom and Dad said stop going to therapy, stop going I did.

My parents weren't being cruel to me; they were just confused. I think that too often we point the finger at others, especially parents, when something goes wrong because we are scared. They made a mistake and they, like so many people, did it out of love. They were afraid I was regressing. They didn't understand the process of therapy; they felt that when improvement had been made, it would remain. They saw me change back, start dieting and dating Kyle, so the conclusion they arrived at was that it wasn't working. Their logic was to pull me out before it got worse. I remember the conversation we had; it was explosive. They expressed how well I was doing, that I was developing confidence, that I was looking at choices in life, not fixating on Kyle's choices, his needs. I became defensive, telling them that they did not understand; that I loved him, he understood me, supported me; that he was not a bad person. My dad looked at me with sadness; he tried to help me see that I wasn't myself anymore, that it was evident in the way I was dressing again, that I never saw my friends anymore. He was right, but I refused to listen. By admitting he was right, I would be wrong. My mom grew very frustrated with me and explained how I was risking my own identity, giving up my independence for him. If someone loves you, they let you be yourself. They were right, but college would be starting again soon, and I needed him there; I couldn't face it alone.

I had decided, however, that even though therapy was over, I would try to do some things to prove to my parents that I was getting better. The first thing I would do would be to enter a talent contest at my high school. Technically, I was still a student until graduation and right before that event, I would sing in front of the whole school. I chose a Crystal Gayle song with an upbeat tempo, and I dressed the part in a long country-style dress. I practiced and felt good about it. On entering the stage I was terrified, but somehow I pulled it off. The kids were clapping to the beat and loving it. I was into it, and I felt like a star. I really sounded good. Sadly, I never know who won; I left before the announcements. I didn't want to know if I lost; it would be too much to face. But I did it—I performed in front of people, and it felt so good. It was a success for me to remember.

Graduation came and went in a fog. I remember having to hold back the tears as I heard my name called. I was done with high school; it was over. Though I felt I hadn't learned a thing that would help me make it, it was behind me at least. All those painful years were over and wasted.

Now it was summer, and although classes were 8 weeks away, it was time to make some other changes. I needed to get a new job, one that would pay me more than I earned at the movie theater. I needed to find myself, whoever that was, and it was time to start fresh. What I was doing wasn't really all that fresh, however, it just looked different. Perhaps the best way to describe it would be to paraphrase a saying I once heard—that insanity is when you do the same thing over and over and expect to get different results. In a similar way, I continued to keep doing new things, but what I didn't realize was that even though what I was doing was new, without a change within myself nothing would change. Sure, some progress had been made in therapy but not nearly enough. I had had a lot of damage to my ego, and if I thought things were really different, then I was in denial again. I felt like I could take on the world. "Okay, I'm learning disabled; now that I know what is wrong everything will get better, I'm cured! Now it's time to celebrate, back to the heavy drinking, back to starving myself, and maybe, just maybe, I will become a country singer."

I found a new job; after all, to my way of thinking at the time that would mean a new life. I broke up with Kyle again. After all, I might meet someone else at my job. I worked as a hostess at a local restaurant. It was the first interview I had, and once more my gifts of charming people and hiding my inabilities secured me the job. It was the most boring job I ever had; furthermore, I had to seat people using a very complicated seating system. I would get it mixed up a lot, and the waiters and waitresses would get so angry with me—all but one, Ted, who really liked me—for reasons that weren't all that helpful. He wanted to date me. Ted was a senior at the university; he was cute, and I was lonely. He was the biggest womanizer I probably ever met, but at 18 I knew nothing, or maybe I just didn't care. He knew I had a lot of pain inside; he also knew I had a major weakness for alcohol. I didn't really care a bit about him; he was simply another challenge, one I knew I could master. It was a very unhealthy way to find some sense of success but a very easy one. I learned that summer that I could have just about anyone I wanted and I began to become the thing I detested, one of those girls so many other girls hate. I would go to parties, flirt with every guy who I thought was cute, and get so drunk I would dance on tables on request. But it was me who hated me more than anyone; I was creating an outward reason to hate myself.

If you hate yourself, it is easy to be destructive. It is even easier to do things and convince yourself they are accomplishments when they really aren't. And if you drown yourself in alcohol, you can always blame it on being drunk. I knew exactly what I was doing before I even picked up the bottle, I just wasn't willing to deal with why I was doing it. The fact that I wanted to have control was all I needed. In thinking back on it now, I must have been a very lucky girl. The things that could have happened to me hadn't, at least not yet, but in time my luck would run out.

That job and that relationship with Ted didn't last long; I didn't want either of them. So it was time to move on. I began to feel bad about my promiscuity. In 1 month, I had managed to seduce and dump three guys. I always made sure I did the dumping; I could never have handled the rejection. I became careless, driving recklessly, drinking excessively, not showing up at home until the early morning hours. I was out of control and didn't even know why. After a month, I became more sullen, but I began to see what I was doing. I became depressed and insecure again. I had to correct this mess, and my old boyfriend Kyle was one way to do just that.

I cared for Kyle, probably because he had as much hidden pain as I did. I always wanted it to work with him—perhaps that is why I kept trying for so long, but he had so many problems and he took them out on me. It was more than I could handle for any length of time. But still I kept trying to fix him; he was another challenge for me, one I thought I could achieve. I thought I could make him better, then he would in turn help me get better. That is not the way it worked out, however; that's never the way it works. You can't change someone; they have to want to change and do it on their own. I would have to go through much more pain, as would he, before we figured out the unhealthy nature of our relationship.

One of the conditions of our getting back together was that I had to quit my job and move out of my parents' house. So I complied. I started first by getting a new job. It was at another restaurant, and again, it was the first place I went to. I got the job right on the spot. I started out as a hostess there, but it was a different system and I had a wonderful supervisor. She was so sweet and so patient. She loved how I was with the customers; the customers loved me, too. I was so energetic and friendly. I quickly moved in that job from hostess to cocktail waitress, and again I was a success. They had a great system for orders; I didn't have to write out the whole word; they used a code system. I memorized it, and when I had trouble, the bartenders (who were guys) never minded helping me.

I told no one that I had a learning disability, and it was lucky for me that the system was such that it was not a big problem. The people were more than helpful and my strengths were emphasized; my ability to work well with people and my lightening-speed actions were valued. They thought I was a nice addition to the restaurant team, and they were a nice addition for me. I was such a good cocktail waitress that I was soon made a luncheon waitress, at which I also excelled. I did have a little trouble taking orders, but again, the people on board were so kind that they worked with me. The help I needed was natural to the staff; they just seemed to accommodate me. If they couldn't read my writing, they would simply ask what it said, and they teased me that maybe I should become a doctor.

The new semester was under way; it was fall and the energy from all of the students around me was an inspiration to me. I had support services and was taking remedial classes to help me with reading, writing, and study skills. I was also taking voice class, tap dance, and family health for a total of 5 credit hours. I was going to classes daily and doing well in three of them. Tap dance, however, was another story. I did nothing but make a complete fool out of myself. I just could not follow the oral instructions. When I was told to go right, I would go left. When I was asked to shuffle, I could not remember what that term and all of the others meant. It was a disaster, and the instructor was not helpful at all. I soon just stopped going. I was too embarrassed to face everyone who was succeeding. But that was okay because I was getting an A in voice class, and I was actually passing health, at least with a D. I was going to make it.

Kyle was growing increasingly impatient with me. I was having too much success: Work was great, I was making friends, and he didn't like it one bit. He gave me an ultimatum: I had to choose between the job or him. I chose the job, although it broke my heart that I had to choose at all. I wasted no time in getting a new boyfriend, David, who was to be the best boyfriend I ever had at that stage of my life.

David was attractive, active like I was, and a senior at the university. We got along great. We started out as friends and shared many thoughts about our lives. I was feeling really good about things. I also made another decision, which was that I wanted to go forward and have my own apartment. I could afford it; I was making good money at the restaurant, and I knew a girl who wanted a roommate. My parents wanted nothing to do with it and told me that they wouldn't help at all, but that was fine. I was having success; I could do it. Little did I know that by taking on too much at once I would eventually destroy the success I had been building for myself. I wanted independence too badly; I didn't plan carefully. I jumped in impulsively and would suffer the consequences.

Soon, I moved into my own place. The apartment was very close to campus. I could ride my bike, which I did, stay out as late as I wanted, which I did, and start taking regular classes. What a great way to feel like I was fitting in! I could forget I had learning disabilities; I was doing everything everyone else was. It was soon to be my third semester (officially, anyway) but really only my second because I had withdrawn from my first. I had not done very well the first semester of my return after diagnosis. I did well in voice class and reading: I received an A and a B respectively, so I was feeling really good about these, but I got a D in family health, and an F in tap dance. Probably, had I done what I was told by my disability services counselors and disclosed my disability to the professors, I would have gotten accommodations for extended test time. If I had had a quiet room to take the test in, note takers, and a tutor, I'm sure I would have done better, but I didn't want the professors and the other students to think I was trying to get away with something. And I didn't want to admit I needed any more help. I wasn't mature enough to know that everyone needs help from time to time.

Spring semester got a lot tougher. I had to take remedial composition class, introduction to psychology, and oral communication, but the one I hated the most, ironically, was pipe organ lessons. My parents had made a deal with me; they would pay for my college classes if I would take pipe organ lessons. Little did they know that the teacher abused me emotionally for my inability to read the notes.

This semester really got me down; I did well in composition and it was a pass/fail class with a great instructor. I had a lot of one-on-one work, just like in reading. But in the other classes I was expected to perform just like all the other students, which was justified. In the organ class, a music class, which had in the past been my talent and my strength, I couldn't do what the professor wanted of me. It was too confusing; I had to remember the stops, when to pull them, how to set up this complicated musical instrument. Why couldn't I just play an instrument? What was wrong with the traditional way I used to play the organ? What was giving me the most trouble was the sequencing. I just could not remember how to do it; there were too many steps to operating the instrument and no strategy for learning it. I remember a conversation with my organ teacher. He told me that although I may have had talent, I would go nowhere if I couldn't read the notes. He informed me that I was obviously not trying hard enough, not practicing. I just didn't care. In some ways he was right; I was forced to take the class, and I didn't tell him about my learning disabilities. How could he know I had a sequencing disability if I didn't inform him? But I could not see that yet; my lack of maturity would stop me from seeing it. I just looked at him, thinking, out of anger—but not saying the words—what a stupid snob; he knew nothing about me, he lost me completely, I wasn't going to pay any attention to this man, I wouldn't listen. So with that I quit going to class; I just wouldn't show up. That way, I thought, I wouldn't fail for being stupid, I would just fail for being lazy and unmotivated. I started having delusions of grandeur. I would laugh inside, thinking

I had won; he would show up for class and I would not be there, serves him right. I refused to let my parents learn that I had been missing class; I got my grades sent to my apartment. Somehow, life wasn't real; it was not really me living this life, it was someone else. So I slid by. I began skipping psychology class (I was failing anyway) and I rarely attended oral communication. The only class I felt obligated to go to was composition, and the only reason I felt this way was that I liked the instructor.

Reality hit when I realized that I was failing again. I knew why, I just didn't know what to do about it. No one offered me any guidance; I was just lost. I had not been taught about self-advocacy so I didn't have the skills or the self-esteem to seek help. Asking for help to me would make me appear weak or dim. I kept hearing this comment over and over in my head: "You're not stupid, even Einstein had a learning disability." Then I would hear my inner voice say, "Well then, if I'm so smart, why do I feel so dumb?" Maybe my life was meant to be like this; maybe I'd never achieve my goals. But I knew there was something out there, I couldn't see myself 10 years or 20 years later having achieved nothing, and at that time motherhood to me didn't account for much in terms of success. Besides, what if I had another me? It was as if there was this incredibly successful person, this highly motivated person who wanted to get out but just didn't know how.

My thoughts, my actions, my relationships all began to revolve around me finding myself. I began to question everything, far more than I had always done. I always questioned life, but now it was more introspective. I guess I had picked up enough in Psychology 101 to be dangerous, at least to myself. My life had always been confusing; I never knew what to do, most things I did were out of impulse, and out of not knowing how to control my impulsiveness. Actually, I couldn't control anything but the destruction I would cause for myself, and after I succeeded in creating harm, I would end up losing over and over again.

I hadn't told David about my learning disability or the fact that I was failing in school. It was too embarrassing. He thought I was bright, beautiful, and a lot of fun to be around. He loved me for who he thought I was but he didn't know who I really was. I hated being phony, not telling the truth about myself, but how could I? I thought he would decide he didn't want anything to do with me. After all, who wants a girlfriend who can't do some of the simplest things in life?

As our relationship developed, I began having more and more self-doubt. I began to feel like my whole life was a mistake; suicide ideation became a predominate factor. I became more and more self-destructive. Drinking wasn't just something I did in the evening anymore—anytime was a good time to drink. There was a time at David's apartment complex that I stood on the railing of the four-story building and threatened to jump, crying hysterically, completely out of control. The alcohol always created more problems. I began to indulge in harming my body again, too: undereating; exercising too much; laying out in the sun every day; and staying up as late as any human could do for days at a time, not sleeping at all. Of course, what I didn't know then was that this behavior was a strong indication of what would become another diagnosis for yet another hidden disability: bipolar disorder.

Those self-destructive behaviors and thoughts were so out of control that I began to sabotage my own life. I began to fight with my sweet boyfriend, a guy who used to bake me pies and leave them at my apartment as a surprise. He was so attentive and compassionate, not an egotist, a genuine person. I began to push the wrong buttons with him, talking about religion, and trying unknowingly to provoke a fight. And worse, I began to see my old boyfriend Kyle again, taking unnecessary risks behind David's back. I craved Kyle's instability, his moodiness, and his control over me. Kyle was predictable. I knew that he knew better than anyone who I was and what I was all about. Kyle had good qualities, most everyone does, but for a young girl with very low self-esteem and very severe learning disabilities, with the mood swings of a roller coaster, he was not the best pick for me, nor was I for him.

Kyle was a very convincing person, and although I told him I only wanted to be friends, that quickly changed, and I was drawn back into a helpless situation of letting someone else tell me who I was and what I was all about. It is easier when you feel worthless to let someone else run your life. The feelings of failure are lessened when you take on someone else's image of you; I could be everything for him; the rest of the world would not matter, and I would only have to prove myself to one person. Of course, to do this I had to break up with David; it broke his heart, and inside it broke my heart more. I knew it was wrong; I knew it was David who I loved, but I just couldn't let him know who I really was.

Over the next month, Kyle and I became very close again. School didn't matter any more; our relationship took precedence. We began to discuss staying together forever, and before we knew it, that decision was made for us. I was pregnant. I didn't want a baby. It was a surprise for both of us; I had been on the pill, but with all the drinking and irresponsible behavior, I forgot to take a few of them. We had to figure out what to do, and of course our parents were outraged and very disappointed. My parents begged me not to marry him. Both sets of parents came around, however, and offered us their support. But I wouldn't listen, the last thing I wanted was to be dependent on my parents. It wasn't right, and I couldn't admit that the offer they gave me to live with them and have the baby was, to me, denigrating.

Kyle and I had already finished the spring semester and summer was well under way. I had achieved a 0.9 GPA that semester, but it didn't matter. I wasn't college material. I was just too dumb; it was time to move on. We had already decided we both needed a change. He couldn't stand the town we lived in; there were too many memories for him to deal with. Any restaurant I may have gone to with David or Juan, any time we would pass a place I had been with them, he would become angry and tell me to put my head down and not to look.

We made a decision: We would move, start fresh, and everything would be different. He would be easier to be around, and I would belong completely to him. So off we went—after a quick marriage ceremony by the judge, we rented a moving van and headed for Dallas. That move was hard on me; I was sick most of the time, it was hot, and I didn't have any air conditioning in my car. I was driving alone, following him in the van. When we got to Dallas, we had to put the furniture in storage for awhile and live at his sister's place for a couple of weeks. I realized then that I had made a major mistake as he began to direct me to lift boxes and help move furniture without giving any care to how ill I was feeling. But misgivings diminished because as quickly as he expressed his anger, he apologized for his behavior.

We had many episodes like this; he was unpredictable and that was scary. I was never sure how to say things to him; one minute he'd love me and the next he hated me. His expectations of me were beyond what I could do; he wanted me to be his wife, his friend, his lover, his mother, his father, his child, himself. He wanted me to be all his, no one else's.

Like it was in high school, my friends had to be approved by him first. He then decided to continue his work on teaching me how to walk, talk, and dress the way he wanted. In other words, he wanted to recreate me to his own liking, and now because I was his wife, he felt he could and he was determined that he would. It was okay, though, at least for a while, because I hadn't done a very good job up to this point. I had messed up my entire life; I couldn't get it right, so maybe I was a screw up and he could teach me. He was, after all, raised in a family with money and prestige, he must know what he was talking about. He must be right, though deep down I resented every change he demanded.

His demands were not my biggest concern at this point, it was finding a job, and somehow we both got lucky in this area. We met a person who owned a baby store and a bank. He went to work at the baby store as a stockroom person; I went to work there as a sales girl. Of course that didn't last long, not because I couldn't do the job, but because I just kept fainting while on my feet. Luckily I was blessed with yet another job opportunity at a bank. I was always getting jobs easily; it was getting beyond the initial hire that I had trouble with. Once I got into a job, my learning disabilities usually became very noticeable to others. If I didn't tell anyone about it, however, they certainly would have thought I was just making mistakes.

In my new position I was to be a drive-up teller: great job for someone who had only attained a fourth-grade math level. But actually, it was easy: The steps were all simple; all the materials were right there, and they encouraged me to take my time, within reason of course. I had a very helpful boss, and she was the first person I disclosed my learning disability to. Her response was very positive. She didn't see it as a problem; instead, she just decided to spend a little extra time teaching me the steps. A month later I had it down and encountered very few problems. I know that if more people were like this supervisor, many people with learning disabilities would have opportunities for success in their jobs. It doesn't really take a lot of effort to help someone with learning disabilities, just some patience, understanding, and an open atti-tude (see Chapter 9 on tips for how employers can help employees with learning disabilities). A handful of supervisors I worked with over the years, along with lessons I learned in my studies, would eventually show me how to teach others what is helpful in supervising people who disclose their hidden disabilities.

My life became more and more difficult as time rolled on. Fortunately, my job was great, but my relationship with Kyle was worsening. He changed jobs several times, and his constant demands were almost more than I could handle. We were both so young and so insecure. I had a very difficult time managing everything. I was ignorant about money, so was he; I was unable to review information we needed for our lives because of my lack of reading comprehension. This was a lot to cope with when there is more to take care of than yourself. I'll never forget trying to fill out an application for a credit card; it was so painstaking. I cried trying to understand what they were asking of me. I didn't know where to go for help, so I'd leave it to him to do. He would get so frustrated with me, tell me how stupid I was, and quickly complete the form.

At that time I could understand why he became annoyed, though his reactions and behaviors were not appropriate. I felt I was a mess. I felt I couldn't do much of anything right. I felt that I messed up almost everything in some way. Kyle wanted his meals on time, and I was never on time; he wanted me to be home at a certain time, and that was nearly impossible, especially when I'd get lost going home, which happened more than once. He was just demanding, and I couldn't keep it all straight. I feared for what life would be like when the baby arrived.

I remember coming home from work one night. I had 10-hour days because of the commute. I was exhausted and not feeling well at all. He had decided for the first time to make me some dinner. Unfortunately, he made me something with an odor that made me so ill I couldn't eat. I sat there looking at that food. He lost control and began yelling at me, telling me how unappreciative I was, how worthless, and that I was a "bitch." He knocked me out of my chair. Tears welled up in my eyes; his anger was worsening day by day. I got up and tried to walk by him but he grabbed my arm and pulled me in front of him, demanding me to sit back down. He told me that I was not to ever walk out on him. I remember shaking and having this overwhelming terror enter my mind. I sat back down. A couple of hours later, he came over to me with a glass of milk and a banana, hugged me, and told me he was sorry—he had "lost his cool" and it wouldn't happen again. I wanted to believe him, but he had apologized so many times before, and nothing had really ever changed.

During this time, I struggled with continuing to read to myself when no one was around. I didn't want him or anyone to know how very hard it was for me. I used the techniques I had been taught in remedial reading; the phonics, the ruler under each line to keep words from moving, the magnifying glass to make the print larger, the variation of light to help reduce the glare, all of these things with agonizingly slow results. Sometimes I would throw the book at the wall, screaming at myself as loudly as I could, calling myself the same names kids called me when I was little. I couldn't drink to suppress the pain because I knew it would hurt the baby. After I calmed down, however, I began to recognize this was a problem. And because I wasn't using a substance to help me cope (or so I thought), I realized I needed to set up a way to deal with this. I refused to let this problem rule my life; I had to find a better way. As much as I hated it, it was one step I had to do to get there; I had to keep trying.

We spent 6 months in Dallas. I was making $800.00 a month in 1982, which was pretty good, and it paid most of the bills. My husband wasn't faring very well, however, and we were concerned about what would happen after the baby was born. But instead of looking for a better job, Kyle would just sit at home and watch music videos on cable television. He had a sense of security that his parents would always help us that annoyed me. I hated that feeling. I don't like being taken care of; that would prove I was truly helpless. When that happened, I felt like I had no reason to go on. I voiced my concern to my parents, and my father offered Kyle a job back in our old hometown. My dad was a chief mechanical engineer for a well-known bread company, and he put in a good word for him. Kyle's job would be delivering bread. The pay and benefits were great; the hours were not so great. The good news, at least for me, was that we would move back home where he would start his job and I would have the baby and start another new life.

We got a nice townhouse that I kept in meticulous shape, and I served our meals on time every day. He liked that, but he hated his job. The early 4:00 A.M. wakeup was more than he could handle.

He quit after 4 weeks. He got a job at a gas station instead; I went into premature labor and delivered our son 5 weeks early. It was a shock to both of us, but after 28 hours of hard labor, our baby was fine, at least at first, but later I would learn he really wasn't fine. He didn't suck well, he didn't respond to touch like most babies, and he seemed easily agitated. We wrote this off to his being premature, but it was more than that; soon we would discover just what was in store for our child and us.

The stress of the baby, the lack of income, and my frustration with staying home became too much for both of us. Kyle didn't want me to work, but I had to, and more important, I wanted to work. So it was decided: I would work as a receptionist somewhere. For me it was easy because it would be routine, not a tough job. It would entail little or no math, lots of greeting people (which I was good at), and managing a telephone system. If I could play the organ as well as I did, certainly I had the coordination to handle a telephone system.

Again the job search was easy; I got my job the first week and the first interview I went on. It was a good job with a Fortune 500 company. I had a decent salary, benefits, and great hours. My job was a blessing; it was a dream come true. I was lucky to have a great supervisor. He was a perfect boss, a true gentleman. He respected me, and he treated me like a daughter. At that time, this was just what I needed. He was honest, caring, and understood my problems. I decided (because I trusted him) to tell him about my learning disabilities. I didn't have to tell him more than once; he never forgot it, and he didn't let it stop him from giving me opportunities to do more and more. Of course this job was not difficult, and everyone really cared about me. I worked hard, and it was appreciated.

Unfortunately, being back in our hometown had its price. Kyle's possessiveness grew stronger. His insecurity increased as soon as I began to work, and my stress over keeping him happy became difficult and upsetting. Kyle's physical force and lack of emotional control became more pronounced, and Justin, our baby, was not reaching any developmental milestones. He'd rock in his crib for hours, he wouldn't play with his toys much, he wouldn't walk, he wouldn't crawl, he wouldn't smile much; mostly he just wanted his bottle.

I remember watching Justin one night when he was a 1-year-old. He was sitting on the floor, toys all around him. He just stared into space, not doing anything, not even trying to move around much. He had one bear he loved; it was always with him. Justin was a beautiful baby with big saucer blue eyes and blond hair; people would stop me all the time and tell me how beautiful he was. But that was not enough, sure he was beautiful, but I knew firsthand that looks only get you in the door; you have to prove yourself beyond that, and he was likely going to face the same fate. I had caused this, I knew I had. I had passed on to him something bad; a gene that would cause him as much if not more pain than I had experienced. Watching him, I knew that my child didn't have a chance unless I took drastic measures. I was not going to let my life and his fall apart, that spark of determination began to rise in me again.

I was approaching 2 years in the job, and I had learned a lot about myself and about enhancing my skills. I was in the right environment: a desk at the top of the stairs, which was secluded from all other distractions except a customer and the telephone. I had developed a system, a sequence on how to do my job. I even conjured up the courage to leave Kyle and take my baby and be independent. After all, I was almost supporting the three of us anyway. So I left. I left a new home, nice furnishings, and filed for divorce. I wanted out, and I didn't even want alimony, which in my mind would have made me feel that I was dependent. No, I only asked for $140 a month in child support and not a dime or anything else from him. I just didn't care; I only knew I didn't want any more pain for me, my child, or for Kyle; he, too, was suffering.

It wasn't easy being a single mother; I was only 21 at the time and I was very scared about how I was going to manage. I learned to write music (using the little I knew about playing chords on the keyboard) to occupy my lonely nights, and I got a used organ that my parents bought for me. This organ was a dream come true, an outlet for my pain. I couldn't afford to go out much, so I was home most of the time and very restless. I set myself up in a run-down but clean townhouse and worked myself down to 95 pounds (which, of course, to me was great). I worked so much and was under so much stress that the weight simply fell off.

I was reaching some of my goals: I was working on math, reading, writing, and using some store-bought workbooks targeted for elementary school-age students. I was working out an hour every day of the week in my garage, eating little to save money (and to keep the weight off); I was focusing on my work and on my child. I did fairly well; I had some help from my parents who bought me groceries occasionally or helped with my car insurance. My checkbook was a mess, but fortunately for me, my mom would help straighten it out. My life was simple; I didn't try to complicate it with debt or relationships. Sure, I dated occasionally and of course all the wrong guys. But that was okay; I didn't want any of them anyway. I just wanted to occupy my time and to prove to myself that I could have someone if I really wanted to. Of course, at that time, I didn't think about why I picked guys who were messed up. Now I know it was because my self-esteem was so low.

Sadly for me, I was about to go through a traumatic event that would alter the way I viewed other people and myself for many years. One of the guys I dated at that time turned out to be a very toxic individual. I saw controlling behaviors in him very similar to those of my ex-husband. I had to tell him that I couldn't see him any more, and he took it very personally. Subsequently, 2 weeks after we broke up, he took control and he raped me. He made a forced entry into my apartment; I was asleep in my room, and there

I was tormented for 3 hours. He told me to stay quiet, or he would kill my son if he awakened. It was the most horrifying night of my life.

A bigger monster than me had arrived, only this monster would set loose all the other monsters I had hidden away. This monster would push me into a shallow, lonely hole in my mind. I was being controlled again. Now I was really stupid, I thought to myself, not just academically but in all aspects of life. Now I had really screwed everything up. Now I couldn't control anything in my life. I was a miserable failure with school, a failure with my child, with men, and with my life.

I didn't know what to do the night I was attacked. After he left, I couldn't think clearly; a million thoughts were running through my head—I was in physical and emotional pain. I didn't know who to reach out for, so out of desperation and panic I called my ex-husband. When I called him and told him what had happened, it was well after 3:00 A.M. He told me he was sorry but that I should have known something like this would happen one day. His words, as cruel as they were, had occurred to me, so I accepted his comments and sank even deeper. He told me he would be over in a couple of hours because he was at work. So I waited. I climbed into the shower and cleaned off my attacker's filth, feeling certain that if I turned him in, I would be the accused.

After some time, I decided to start seeing my ex-husband again. He stayed with me almost every night, and I felt safe. I began therapy right after the rape, but I just couldn't hold it together. My performance started to slip and I fell further and further behind in my work. My boss noticed, as everyone noticed, that I was acting differently, but no one knew why. My happy personality was gone. I was trying to hold up after the attack but instead I was remembering all of my failures and feeling the pressure from everyone. I didn't tell my parents about it, and I kept the bruises hidden. I was too embarrassed; they didn't really notice that anything was wrong. They were so busy trying to help my brother who at that time was having personal problems.

Soon it was more than I could handle. I couldn't sleep unless Kyle was over; I couldn't eat; I quit exercising; and most frightening of all, I quit dreaming. Going to the grocery store terrified me, everywhere I went I would think he was there. I started telling myself how stupid I was, how incapable I was, that there would be no way out of this pain. I thought that the rape was just a reminder to me that I had made yet another mistake, and it opened up flashbacks of what had happened to me as a child. I was nothing more than an idiot, a marionette for men. So I stole sleeping pills from my mother's house, bought a bottle of Jack Daniels, and planned to drive to my secret place in the woods. But before I did, I decided to go by my psychologist's office one more time. Somewhere inside I wanted help; I didn't really want to die.

I was lucky that night; her light was on in her office, and she was alone. I entered; she could tell I was distraught as I told her about my plan. I told her how I hated myself: I was hopeless, I was dumb, and now I was afraid. I was never afraid like this before, nothing stopped me, and I had always found another way out, but now I was terrified. I wanted to die. I hated the world, it hurt me, no one understood me, and no one cared. The world was filled with bad and uncaring people. I remember gazing out the window, feeling paralyzed. "I want to die, all my life I've failed, I can't seem to get things right. I serve no purpose," I told my therapist. Her words to me were like words from an angel as she leaned forward and looked at me. I could tell she really cared. She talked me into going to the hospital. My sister and my ex-husband helped by caring for my son.

While I was there, I worked on my weight and learned I was anorexic. I worked on my pain from the assault and the painful childhood memories of that other assault. I worked on my relationship with my family (even though my parents could not bear to see me in this way and they only visited one time; it was too painful for them). I also worked on my helplessness with my ex-husband, but I avoided discussing my learning disabilities. It was so much to deal with—what I thought of as the stupidity factor. They couldn't help me with that in therapy, or so I thought. I had to keep that mask on, hide that flaw.

Eventually, my grandiosity began to return; my resilience would prevail. I wanted out. Although it had been only 3 weeks, it was time to go. I had noticed all of the other patients around me; many of them seemed to have given up. I couldn't be like them—I was different. I would fight and not give up. I just couldn't—the call to survive was too strong. I had to find my own way to identify what I was feeling inside myself. My grandmother had told me years ago that I would be someone special one day. I could not give up; I knew somehow that she was right. I didn't want to be like this. I wanted more. I owed it to my son. I owed it to me. I remember the positive messages my teachers, my family, and my friends had given me in the past. This trove of messages was like discovering gold; I pulled out the pieces I needed to gain the strength to fight. I convinced the doctors that I was cured; I was almost euphoric, on a high, my manipulation skills had returned. I wasn't taking any drugs. I refused them, the depression lifted, and I was ready to take on the world.

I returned to work, but it wasn't easy. People were different to me, and things were different. It didn't seem fair. I sensed the distance, and within weeks, I was told my job was being eliminated. I don't know to this day how many of them found out where I really was. We tried to cover it up, and the only people who knew were my boss, the general manager, and the corporate human resources department. Maybe they did learn about it, maybe my ex-husband told them what happened, but I was now an outcast, and my life was about to get a lot tougher. My boss cried as he told me my job had been eliminated. I loved that man; I don't think he ever knew how much his kindness meant to me.

So here I was, a single mom without a job, few skills, and an uncertain direction. I had no one to guide me, no one to help me, but that didn't stop me from trying. I wanted more for my son and me and I had to find it. I had to get away from everything. So I made a very difficult decision to move more than 200 miles from where I had been for nearly 10 years. I had to leave my family, my ex-husband, and all the familiar things I had learned were both good and bad behind.

This risk would be one of the best decisions I would ever make in my adult life because it would lead to the greatest successes, things I would never have dreamed possible. But this move led to new challenges for me, new questions I asked myself. What do I do? Should I tell people about my learning disabilities? What risks do I pose for myself? My decision was to avoid telling people about my LD, at least until I got the job and then I would disclose if I had to. But I hoped I wouldn't have to. I didn't want to feel helpless; I had been there once and I didn't like it at all; I had to be strong.

There were other factors that were influencing my decision as well, involving my son. I had been told by a group of specialists that my child was mentally retarded with autistic tendencies, but deep down I knew they were wrong. There was just too much going on inside those eyes. I could see it; I just didn't know how to get it out. But how could I, when I wasn't even sure how to get it out of myself? Justin was almost 3 years old when we received this diagnosis. I was devastated. How was I supposed to be able to help him? I could barely help myself. My God, I caused this, I told myself. Maybe it was genetics. Maybe it was because of the abuse inflicted on my body, or maybe it was the highly volatile relationship between his father and me.

The move would be an adventure and it would mark my transition from young adulthood into full-blown adulthood quickly, with limited emotional support. I would learn more in the next few years about being an adult with hidden disabilities, about being a woman, and about being a mother than I had at any other time in my life. I would learn how I could share and help others understand what it takes to survive as a person with severe hidden disabilities, ones that much of the rest of the world don't want to believe exist.

INSIGHTS AND INTERVENTIONS
by Larry B. Silver, M.D.

Although poorly prepared, Veronica was off to college. Her reading, writing, written language, math, and organizational problems were still unrecognized and overwhelming to her. Her first day and registration mirrored the year to come. She lived with fear and with failures. She was lost and confused. As in the past, she felt stupid and had no self-confidence. She continued the theme from high school. She sought out boyfriends who would protect and take care of her, but she always paid a price. She hated being dependent but needed to be this way to survive. It is difficult to imagine what feelings and thoughts were constantly in her head. Perhaps it would have been easier for her if she were not so bright and introspective, but she was. Others could "act out" their needs and never wonder why. She did what she needed to do to survive but never stopped looking into the mirror and seeing what she was doing. Her insight and her inability to do anything differently at the time are so painfully described: "But for a puppet to survive, it has to let its master and controller make its every move; otherwise it does not have the ability to function on its own."

For those educators reading this book, don't let another Veronica get through your classroom without doing something. Try to understand the "why" behind the behaviors. Try to find out why the behavior exists. Remember that a little extra time can reap great rewards—not just in improved classroom performance, but in every facet of the student's life now and in the future.

Attending college classes did not work for Veronica. Should she have been surprised? Her learning disabilities resulted in her not being able to read, copy, take notes, or write. Her language disabilities made listening to lectures and understanding what was said more than difficult. Her attention-deficit/hyperactivity disorder resulted in her being distracted by all activities around her. She tried desperately to act like a student by trying to study and to prepare for examinations, but how do you study when you cannot read? How do you review class notes when you cannot listen and write at the same time; thus, your notes are limited? How do you learn material when everything is disorganized? How do you do college math when you don't know elementary school math? Again, all she could conclude was that she was unintelligent. Again, she questioned her purpose in life.

At last, when Veronica was 18, a teacher responded the right way. She was failing psychology yet seemed to know the material. This teacher took the time to look over her notes and to discuss her problems. For the first time, the possibility of a learning disability was mentioned. This teacher has to be considered the most critical person in starting the process of turning Veronica's life around. But the road ahead was not an easy one.

Psychoeducational testing showed that she was bright, with excellent listening and talking skills. Her reading skills were at the second-grade level, spelling at the third-grade level, and math was equally low. She had fine motor difficulties that made handwriting slow and poor. Her ability to get her thoughts onto the page was limited. How did she get through 12 years of education and graduate from high school this way? Unfortunately, this is not an anomaly, but happens all too often to individuals with learning disabilities. Although it is not unusual, it is preventable. (In Chapter 9, Veronica provides a wealth of information on what to look for during various stages of an individual's life and explains how to help individuals who may have hidden learning disabilities.) We can only imagine what a different life Veronica might have had with early recognition and intervention.

When the test results were discussed with Veronica and her mother, she felt more pain for her mother than for herself. She could not let herself think that anyone other than the school system had missed what was going on. Instead, she had to blame herself for the embarrassment and pain she caused her mother. Perhaps it was too overwhelming for her to realize that her mother needed to experience her own feelings of anger and guilt as did Veronica and that this was okay. Also, it would have been helpful if the people communicating the test results had explained the findings in a thorough and sensitive manner.

As her life progressed, her relationships with significant men in her life reflected her own changes in self-esteem. When she felt good about herself, as when she was in therapy, she distanced herself from unhealthy relationships. When she returned to feeling slow and incompetent, she reconnected with dependent, unhealthy relationships. Her young adult years reflect this theme over and over.

After her diagnosis, Veronica returned to classes but did not feel safe disclosing her learning disabilities to her faculty. Those readers with learning disabilities understand her problem. Knowing when it is safe to disclose is so difficult. Who will be accepting and who will respond negatively? Many social biases still surround the types of disabilities that Veronica has. Her drop in grades, her return to alcohol and drugs, her eating disorder, and her thoughts of suicide all indicate that she suffered a serious self-esteem problem at this time. She also experienced what later would be understood as a manic episode, part of another diagnosis not yet recognized, bipolar disorder (formerly called manic-depressive disorder).

The less she thought of herself, the more she needed to be dependent on a boyfriend. She needed him to take care of her and to protect her. She needed feedback from someone that she was worthy of attention, even if the attention was negative. Thus we read of her marriage to her old boyfriend Kyle, her move, and her pregnancy. The abuse she experienced became both physical and emotional. Though she moved again and found some success with a job, it did not help. The negative, destructive relationship continued. She left, and faced the world of being a single mother. Sadly, her internal turmoil resulted in the same pattern of male relationships. Then, the ultimate physical and psychological abuse occurred. She was raped. In desperation, she returned to her former husband. She needed to be taken care of and protected but she was not protected emotionally. Thoughts of suicide increased, and she was finally hospitalized.

The time in the hospital appears to have been helpful. When she left, she decided to move away from her family and friends and toward another new adventure. This reminds me of the way she survived her childhood trauma, by moving. Each move brought new hope for something to be different. With each move, however, she brought herself—her nightmare—with her.

6

SOUR GRAPES

NAVIGATING THE WORKING WORLD

I felt like I was
sinking in quicksand.
My mind was racing a
mile a minute:
How could I explain
this in a
job interview?

I wonder sometimes if each person experiences tremendous fear but then keeps it hidden so well that it isn't even recognizable to him- or herself. Obviously everyone—especially by the time they reach young adulthood—has experienced at least some fear. For adults with learning disabilities in particular, the fear from past years becomes like a growing mold, one layer of unidentifiable growth on top of another. You see, when you know from past experience that you have been made fun of, that you are not able to compete on the same level as others but that you intellectually function at their level, it creates difficulties in every aspect of your life. I was to find this particularly true in my young adult years, and to find out that I could not run from my disabilities or past.

Now I was in a new town miles from home, starting over, or so I thought. In my case, moving was necessary for two reasons. One, I wanted to get services for my son, Justin. In the place I had lived previously, there was nothing for him. Two, I needed to escape because of the man who had raped me. I just couldn't stay in the same town with this man; fear did play a factor in my decision to move.

The first thing I had to do was to get a job that would support my son and me, and for the first time, I experienced difficulties getting a job. Think back for a moment of a time when, to gain employment, you had to pass an aptitude test. Then think how you would feel if you learned that that aptitude test would determine your ability to do tasks or skills that weren't even used on the job. I had this experience. Ironically, I applied for a job as a receptionist that I should have gotten. My past experience demonstrated my capabilities but I didn't get it because my math and punctuation skills were below the employer's standards. So, I had to find a job outside of what I could do well that didn't require testing just so I could support my son and myself.

By now, I had been looking for 2 months, and I was starting to feel overwhelmed. Soon, the money would run out. I had bills to pay; I had a child who depended on me. I just hoped and prayed that I would pass just one test. I was so hurt and angry; I knew I could do those jobs. My interviewing skills weren't enough; half of the time I couldn't even get to the interview unless I passed the test.

It was at this time that I realized I would have to go to a placement agency, one in which the employer would pay the agency if I were hired. In my mind, this indicated still another weakness: I couldn't even find a receptionist job on my own; I needed help. I hated asking for help; needing it must mean that I had more severe disabilities than I had thought. Luckily, I met a woman who worked at the agency who seemed to understand me. I lied to her; I told her that I had test anxiety, not that I had learning disabilities. I couldn't tell her the truth. I feared she wouldn't work with me so I told her I would need to find a job in which a test would not be required. I hated that I was lying. I didn't want to let her down, and she was so nice. But it was critical; I just couldn't risk it. Before long, she had an interview for me with a small, family-owned company in which I talked my way into a job as an accountant's assistant. Of course, I didn't disclose my learning disabilities, I couldn't, and I needed the job. I figured I always had a good work ethic, and after all, this type of job would be a breeze, only adding and subtracting. I could do that with a calculator. Although I was concerned about figuring out percentages, I figured I would find a way somehow. So it was done, my charm got me the job; I was hired on the spot! I remember thanking God for the job and the skill to talk my way into it. I also remember praying that I could manage the job, begging God to grant me a brain, one that would work well.

During the time I was in the process of moving, I had met a nice man. He was actually my ex-husband's cousin. Paul was a real estate broker and knew the city well. I had been told told to look him up so that I would not live in a bad part of town. I had met him once before when I was 16 and had paid no attention then; he was just the older cousin, 7 years my senior. The first time we met, it was at a restaurant where we discussed the city. Paul was handsome and successful; he was outgoing and had a great smile. He offered to help me any way he could, including coming over to help me get settled. That set things up, and within a week of meeting, we began to date. He was refreshing; he never gave me the indication that he wanted to possess me. I didn't quite understand that because most of the guys I dated wanted to possess me at some level. Instead, he gave me space—sometimes too much; I was uncomfortable with that at times. There would be times I would not hear from him for days; this was very strange for me. But I shrugged it off and decided that this must be good; after all, I had tried it the other way and look what good it had done me.

I decided to take my chances with Paul, to take things very slowly and be completely honest with him. I told him all about my past, at least to the level I was able to articulate it. It was very hard to do, but he seemed so open. I told him of my dreams, how I wanted to go back to school one day, and that I was going to look into a system known as vocational rehabilitation (VR) to see if perhaps they could help me get started. I also let him hear a demonstration tape I had made more than a year previously of a song I had written, composed, and sung. Later, he would tell me that he fell in love with me the moment he heard my voice. He said he'd never heard such a powerful, beautiful voice and that he had hoped I would turn that talent into a profession. What he didn't know is that my tough, strong façade was fake and that I was nothing more than a scared little girl who wanted to be loved and cared for. I would have been happy getting my degree, having a career, and staying close to him at all times.

Paul did not seem afraid of my dreams to go back to college; he did not find them ridiculous. On the contrary, he found them alluring; he was very supportive and encouraging. He brought up examples from my past and told me he had never met anyone like me, someone who stood strong and pushed on. I never thought of myself in that way—as a survivor, but he was right. I did pull myself back up time and time again. What Paul didn't know was that I was very insecure and nervous, and that deep down I didn't really believe I had the capability to do much of anything. He didn't know that I felt at any moment as if my world would come crashing down and I would be left standing alone in the rain. He expressed to me that he knew I would be successful. He wasn't overly concerned about what his parents or family would think of our strange relationship; it didn't seem to matter, but in reality it would and did. It would be something that would be a struggle we could never overcome. He was as naïve as I was; he thought I was a goddess, and I thought that with him behind me I really could become something special.

The job I had acquired was a nightmare; anyone who has ever had a bad experience with a boss, anyone who has struggled to survive in a job, will understand. I couldn't figure out the system and to make matters worse, one of the supervisors seemed obsessed with me and would leave notes on my desk with comments about my body that made me feel very uncomfortable. He was coming over to my apartment unannounced and late at night, placing me in a very awkward position, making me feel unsure of myself, and creating flashbacks to the events I had been through with my ex-husband and the man who raped me. I didn't know how to handle him. I felt that I was in a position in which I could not afford to lose my job, so I was nice. Of course, it wasn't until much later that I would realize this was the wrong approach — but I didn't know what else to do. I was barely making it and the last thing I needed was to lose my job. It was a classic case of sexual harassment and I was terrified but also uneducated as to my rights.

Work became like a game; each day I would come in, slap a smile on my face just like when I was in school, play the game of "I like you, too," and pray he would lose steam. If that wasn't bad enough, I had to pretend for my immediate boss that I knew what I was doing on the job and not screw up badly. But hiding my difficulties was no longer an option; I got my first performance review 3 months into the job, and I was placed on probation. I was faced with a decision: I knew I had to tell the owner who hired me about my learning disabilities. After all, what did I have to lose at this point? If I didn't, I would be fired.

Fortunately for me, things worked out, though my supervisor was disappointed that I had not discussed this up front. He told me that he had a child with similar disabilities. We discussed a plan of action for me; I would work more closely with him and set up a system. I would do more data entry, and the other girl in the office would take over the payables; I could still do the receivables. I thought this would take care of the problem. I was relieved that at least I would not have to face two problems on the job. My risk of being fired had now been eliminated, but the man who was harassing me was still a very big concern.

I would like to state that I don't think he should have ever hired me, not because I had LD, but because I had no experience in working this type of job. So essentially we were both at fault. I interviewed well and did not disclose, and he didn't interview well and was not focused on the essential requirements of the job. Regardless of who was right or wrong, he understood to some degree and gave me more training time. For the duration of my time remaining on the job, I did perform much better, but as usual, I was working 10-hour days just to keep up, and sometimes coming in on Saturdays. I still did not understand my own learning disabilities; all I knew was that I couldn't read, write, or do math very well. I had no idea, because no one ever told me, that I had sequencing, short-term, and working memory disabilities. Nor did I know that I had auditory sequential memory disabilities.

One would think I would figure it out, right? After going through so many years of schooling trying to pretend to be normal, I just simply quit trying to figure out what was wrong; it was too painful. It was obvious in my work, however, that I always did things wrong when directions were given orally. It wasn't that I couldn't hear the words or understand that I was being told to do a specific task; it was the order in which I was supposed to do it. I had a severe sequential disability. And if that weren't enough, it didn't occur to me either that it was a learning disability that hindered my ability to retain what names to go look up. I just didn't know enough about my assets and limitations for me to set up systems or to ask for information in a different way. The one thing I did have was a strong work ethic that I got from my parents. I always worked very hard, always came in on time, and always helped others when they needed it. I wanted to do well, but it would eventually become too stressful.

It was difficult enough to balance being a single parent with trying to do a job that was extremely difficult considering the learning disabilities I had, but when you add the sexual harassment issues, it was unbearable. Eventually the signs of stress began to show; I missed some work, slowed down in my performance, and had a great deal of trouble sleeping at night. I told Paul about this man, so he showed up occasionally in an attempt to discourage my supervisor from thinking he could get to me. I also asked a woman to move in with me. I had enough room, and I thought that by having an apartment-mate, it would not only protect me but it also would help with the bills. At first it was helpful, but it was difficult as well; she and I had some differences in the way we did things. She had a child also, and our styles in parenting were very different. She was also quite messy, and that was one thing I could not tolerate—having my very clean, organized, and calm environment destroyed. After 2 months, she had to leave, not just at my request, but at my landlord's, although I was pleased to see her leave because of the chaos. I would lose the extra income and my ability to sleep knowing I was alone in the house, however.

One night while I was up very late I heard a strange noise outside. I looked out my second-floor window to find my boss calling for me to let him in my apartment. I panicked; I was thrown into a frenzy remembering the rape. I called Paul, and he told me to tell him I would call the police if he didn't leave, so I did just that. I opened the window and yelled down at him. But what a price to pay, for I knew he would get even.

The next day I went into work and was hit with the news. I knew when I walked in that morning and passed by the office of the boss and saw this man who had been harassing me all this time sitting there that I was in for a very unfortunate surprise. My boss called me into his office; as I walked in, he walked out glaring at me. He proceeded to tell me I was fired. I was shocked—how could he do this? I knew my performance wasn't terrific but I was doing the job at least in an average manner, or so I had been told the last week.

After long discussion, mostly his, he told me that the reason he was letting me go was because his partner believed I was doing drugs. My reaction was surprising even to me. Somewhere I got the courage and the quick response (not my style) and explained to him that I did not do drugs. I added that when I left, I would go to the hospital for a drug test and it would be negative; then I would find a lawyer to help me. I was so scared. I held back from telling him too much about the harassment; I couldn't—it was his brother who was doing it. The look on his face—I will never forget it. He did not question anything I told him; he only responded by saying, "I didn't know this job was that important to you. We will give it another try." He reneged on firing me right then and there, and I would stay employed for another month. I would then tell them I was resigning.

Fortunately, by the time this occurred, I had accomplished a few things. I had gone to vocational rehabilitation (VR) and was diagnosed again with severe learning disabilities in reading, writing, and math. The memory and sequential learning disabilities were also noted. And to my surprise, a new term was used to describe me that I had never heard of, *attention-deficit disorder*

(ADD), residual type. I was granted support from VR to attend the local community college. This would allow me to start working toward my dreams. Paul and I had also decided to get married.

Finally, my life seemed to be going right. I chose to ignore the signs that Paul, although he cared, was fairly emotionally removed, but that was okay; he didn't beat me, he didn't call me names, he was stable. I was so amazed I had gotten approved for college support. I just couldn't believe it; someone, a group, a government organization, believed in me. Of course, there were requirements I would have to fulfill. I was fortunate, though; my counselor argued on my behalf that I be allowed to take only 7 hours of classes as a trial (VR required 12), but she and I both knew it would take a couple of semesters to achieve a full-load ability. So it was arranged that I would start college in the fall. I wasn't sure how this would happen, but eventually it all fell into place. Paul and I worked out a plan: He wanted me to fulfill those dreams, and he also wanted me to have a baby. I could be a full-time mother and a full-time student, and it would work out fine. And somehow I knew he was right, because I would find a way to do it all. We both knew that if I could get through school, the income I could make would be of tremendous help to our family. It was the smart thing to do as an investment in our future. We would have to make sacrifices for me to not work and go to school full time, but that was okay, I had been so poor for so long, I felt now I could finally let down my guard.

The wedding was beautiful. I hadn't had a wedding nor had Paul. I was in a state of shock as I walked down the aisle, looking ahead at this man who I believed was my knight in shining armor. He was secure in who he was, so outgoing. I was proud of him and honored to be marrying him. That memory stays with me even today, perhaps because it was more my dream than his; perhaps somehow I knew that I had been the one to push the marriage. I had given him an ultimatum. I told him he had to make a commitment or I would walk. Regardless, he did, and I believed that must mean something. The marriage had a lot going against it from the start; it would take a lot of hard work and trust for things to work out, but I was determined, as I believed we both were.

I am sure I did not fulfill the most appropriate of bridal requirements. Honestly, I forgot a lot of things I was supposed to do. Needless to say the wedding was a bit unorganized; I had done 80% of the planning. Fortunately, no one seemed to care; people appeared to be having fun, and I was having the time of my life. I wasn't concerned at all about the status of some of our guests, my husband's family's status. They were upper class, and I was somewhere in the lower middle. Their big, beautiful home in which we had our reception made me feel like I was marrying a prince. Nothing seemed to matter, the fact that my husband's father's sister and her family were absent (my ex-husband's family), that we had many worries that faced us, a new instant family, it would just all work out. Nothing would intimidate me that day; it was the first time I felt sort of normal. The guests didn't know I had a lot of pain wrapped up tight inside. They didn't realize that the 100-pound frame at 5' 5" inches wasn't natural, they only saw me as a bride. It's sad to think how we look for things in life to mask our pain, and in doing so, the consequences can be negative, a lifelong chain of events that create much sadness for all of those involved.

That summer we got settled into our home. My son began to make adjustments and would start an early childhood program for children who were cognitively low functioning and had behavioral problems. We were both starting something new; we would both experience learning such as we never had before. As that fall began, the stress of being a new family began to show. I started learning more about my new wonderful husband whom I adored so much; I drove him crazy by constantly calling him at work and following him around the house. One day, a telephone call came while I was painting the family room; the answering machine picked it up. To my shock, it was a woman; not a client—but someone confirming a bike ride she and my husband were to take in the park that day. I began to shake; I couldn't help but wonder. We had only been married 2 months, what was wrong? What did I do wrong this time? The rage emerged; it grew beyond control. I held it inside until he got home, and then the explosion occurred. He witnessed a highly emotional, raging girl of 23, crying hysterically, yelling out her feelings, thoughts, and innuendoes. He screamed back at me; it was an old girlfriend, nothing was going on, he said. But that made it worse—an old girlfriend! He tried to tell me that she wanted to talk with him about business. I continued to scream irrationally. I imagined this tall, successful woman (which she was) riding in front of him, flashing her "behind." I began to get sick; I ran into the bathroom and looked in the mirror. All I could think of was how very ugly, how very fat I must be. I emerged saying nothing more about it until it happened again.

Things then stabilized some, though I was struggling with balancing school and my son's needs and trying to ease the concerns of my husband, who was scared and feeling helpless from having a child and a wife who both had lots of negative baggage. We would experience many roadblocks, struggles, and difficulties, especially during our first year. He would learn how frustrating learning was for me, and I would learn how frustrated he was with my growing need to have him near me.

Many people believe that it must be very helpful for children with learning disabilities to have a parent who has learning disabilities as well. People would often say to me, "It must make Justin's easier to understand, after all, look how good you turned out. It must give you a sense of hope for him, you must have extreme patience." If only they knew the real truth. I don't know what it is like for someone without disabilities to have a child who has these problems. I wouldn't pretend to know what it feels like, but I can tell you one thing, having more understanding or finding it somehow easier is not always the case. At least it wasn't for me. When Justin got on that bus the first day of school at the age of 3½, I remember saying, "Good, maybe they can fix him." I remember praying that the disability would just work its way out, even though I knew from the time that he was only a few months old that something was wrong. If my LD had not gone away, why would his problems go away, and if life were this difficult for me, then how would life be for him? It was hard for me; of course now I know why, but at that time I really believed it was my fault—that I had passed my learning disability genes to him. And I had not come to any conclusion that there was anything good about having LD and ADHD; I saw it as really all bad. I am sure most parents go through this; they wonder what they could have done differently. I knew what I could have done differently—I could have not gotten pregnant. The guilt was extremely high and my frustration level with Justin was high, not because of his problems, but because of my own. Like so many parents, Paul was trying to do what he thought was right, and even I had very high expectations of Justin. I began to feel that the soft approach I had used with Justin when it was just the two of us had hardened. I had to be like Paul, be tough; after all, he must know what he was doing. Paul did manage to toilet teach Justin at age 3, and that was something I could not do. We put a lot of pressure on him to be better, much better than at the time he was capable of, such as expecting him to be able to ride his tricycle. I mean, how hard can that be, we thought to ourselves. I would watch him with Paul as he pushed Justin on his tricycle, yelling at him to put his legs on the pedals, telling him to move his legs. Hour after hour we'd work on getting Justin's legs to move in the circular motion but he would just sit there repeating in his echolalic language, "Move your legs." Then there was the echolalia altogether; everything we said to him, he would repeat back. I would get too upset with him: I would say, "Justin, you don't need to repeat everything I say." He would respond, "You don't need to repeat everything I say." I would want to sit on the floor and cry. This was all my fault. This beautiful child would have to go through life like I had, only to my fear, much worse; oh—his disabilities seemed so much worse than mine. I worried that I would lose my husband because of this. So it began: We were both much too hard on him.

I think that for Paul, it was particularly difficult. He was 30 before he married; now he had a wife and son. I could sense many times his regret in ever having made this decision. He even voiced it once in a while in so many words, that living with these disabilities was tough. Regardless, I knew I had to stay strong, not give up. My son needed me to be strong, and although inside I was weak, I knew I had to prove to him that despite my severe learning disabilities I had succeeded in my own way and he could, too.

The first semester was an experience I will never forget. I anticipated that I would somehow succeed. Though scared and still unprepared for the demands of college life, I felt I had a little bit more behind me than I did for my first attempt at college. One requirement of VR was that I go through the disability services department; this department would help me to get the accommodations I needed. I was so eager to learn that I was willing to try any suggestion they gave me. The classes were balanced so that I would have an opportunity for success. Sure, at times I felt it was a slow transition, but it would be a transition that would lead me to better things. The classes I took were human services, volleyball, and college reading and study skills. Only two of the classes were highly demanding academically, but I followed the rules: talk with the instructors, get the syllabus in advance, get the textbooks on tape, use the English learning lab for help with reports, and work harder than I ever had before.

I was ready for the challenge; it occurred to me that although I felt I was a failure, I was much more afraid to go back to the real world without preparation. I had already done that and knew how frustrating it could be. I think sometimes that the population of people with disabilities tends to mature a little slower than do those without hidden disabilities. Maybe it's just that we are so frustrated with unsuccessful ventures that we don't really want to grow up; if childhood was difficult, adulthood will most likely be a disaster. So, even though we become adults we are not as responsible, partially because of the need for a high level of knowledge and partially because of fear. In my case, I wanted to crawl back into bed and forget it all, to be a mother and wife and that's all; but the other side of me wanted desperately to get out, to have other experiences in life, to be more well-rounded. I knew I had something to offer; I just didn't know exactly what it was.

As I began learning to study and getting oriented to school and a new life, I began to have this sense of inner strength. I had promised others and myself that I would make it, therefore I must. It was painful to study for hours on hours each night, and during that time, I had to get it all together. I don't think anyone, with the exception of my husband, really realized how hard I had to work. Paul had to tolerate my anger. I would throw the books and cry at the table with frustration, feeling anxiety over an upcoming test. I remember expressing to him how stupid I felt, but holding inside that it was more than just a feeling for me. When I looked at how long it took me to process information and analyzed why, for me being stupid was reality. I pretended to be satisfied with how things were going for me, talking up my success like I believed it, but I knew differently. I had become an actress of sorts, much like when I was a kid. This time, however, it was more dishonest. I was an adult and though I was having success, my monster was still haunting me.

It was hard for me to believe, but I did start doing very well in school. By the end of the first semester I had brought up my grade-point average from a .9 to a 3.3 overall! I was ecstatic; my counselor at school was congratulating my husband, my parents were thrilled, but still inside I was feeling a sense that something was missing. Fine, I had academic success, but I was still me, and I was still struggling. But again I had to keep this feeling hidden. I couldn't let anyone down. I had done that before and it hurt. So I created a plan—one I could not share with anyone. I would keep up with the smiles, keep talking about the success, keep working hard, but watch out! As with most of my life's experiences, I was certain that it was just a matter of time before something would go wrong; I had to be aware of this and keep an eye open at all times, otherwise any problem would be a much harsher reality. Ironically, this pretending kept me going; I wouldn't be called a failure by anyone ever again. But what I didn't know was that my pretending to be successful and happy would have its own price to pay in personal relationships.

Things began to happen to me. I became increasingly angry and agitated. I would look for any sign that Paul didn't love me. Of course, he was doing things to provoke my fears even more. He would have lunches out with old girlfriends that he'd forget to tell me about or invite me to attend. Rather than assuming it was business, I assumed it was because he was embarrassed by me. Instead of seeing his problems as his own, I saw them as a reflection of me, his anger, his lack of patience with Justin—it was all my fault. Anytime anything went wrong, it was my fault. I would find myself going from grandiosity (feeling I could do it all) to extreme sadness (feeling lost and alone). It was as if I was the second hand on a clock that was swinging from the 12 to the 6 and backward up to the 12 and back again to the 6. I had trouble sleeping. Ironically, my lack of sleep was of benefit to me; I spent every night, every weekend, every spare moment I could give studying. I was exhausted, yet I was euphoric.

It is important to mention another significant and charismatic person in my life at that time, Maggie, a community college VR disability services counselor. She had tremendous wisdom about LD. She saw my potential; she saw my raw talent in public speaking and would offer me an opportunity that would lead me to where I am today. Maggie had a gift, and she offered it to me. She took a chance and saved my life, not realizing like the others what this gift she gave me did for my life.

Maggie also taught me how to make it in school by reducing many frustrations that removed my doubt and fear. These tools were critical to my college success. Had it not been for these tips and my following them every semester to the letter, I would still be struggling. Of course at the time I could not see this; it was still very interesting to me that I was succeeding. I had developed a system with Maggie's guidance. During each semester I would implement it and it would allow me success. We would set up a schedule so that I was taking classes with balance: one class that was required and would be difficult, balanced with one I would be likely to manage with little extra assistance. I would also gradually build more hours in each semester as I developed confidence and competence. Both strategies are critical factors in college success for those with learning disabilities.

During the time I was at the community college, I had other events that would challenge my life. By the next semester (which began in February), I had learned that I was pregnant again. Fortunately for me, I had Maggie in my life, who was a wonderful counselor and who did not let my pregnancy influence her decision to keep me funded. She supported me all the way.

I had a beautiful baby girl! Tess came earlier than planned, but I would find a way to make it work. Inside I was almost hoping that I would be satisfied with being a mom and not have this pull to keep going. I was tired and certain that the monster was close, that it would have me soon, but still I kept going.

I set up my life around my darling baby, finishing that semester at home and taking the next semester through television coursework. The barriers became bigger and bigger. The classes were not helpful to me, there was too much focus on reading, and I was unable to ask questions of the professors. Not being able to know who these professors were and what they were all about created stress and a strong anticipation that I would fail. When I thought of failing, sometimes I would hear myself say, "That's okay, it would be over then; you wouldn't have to work as hard." Then other times I heard myself say, "But you'd be a bigger failure than you are today. Everyone would know you're stupid then." Somehow I managed to get through those classes—not well, however. I got Cs in all three classes. I also ran into some new problems—ones that would follow me from here on.

I began to notice the different way I was treated by my husband's family. They didn't have much of an interest in what I was doing. I was so eager to show them what I could do; I wanted them to like me. I didn't realize then that my social skills and self-esteem affected the way I relayed information to them and to some of our friends. I was pretty uptight most of the time, afraid to risk saying anything except to talk about school. I had finally developed success in one part of my life. That success felt great, but I did not know it was inappropriate to talk about one's success all the time; I thought that was a good thing. I knew it was true; I didn't have to quote facts. It gave me something to talk to them about; it was a comfort area. I figured it was better to talk about my success and excitement about school than to keep my mouth shut or to tell them how I really felt inside. But how could they understand? People who don't have or don't know about these disabilities don't understand (not because they don't want to) what struggles we face with our inner selves. It would be easy to assume that people such as me are a bit too egocentric, narcissistic, or idealistic. On the surface, it looks that way. Perhaps though, if you look a little deeper you may see a complex, loving, and curious person who would welcome your interest and your knowledge. But, instead, I felt that my husband's siblings looked on me as a social rube.

I can see how easy it is for someone with LD and ADHD to give up. It hurts so much to try so hard every day, sometimes relearning what you learned the day before because you forgot it all, and comparing yourself to others and realizing you are different! If you fail, then you don't have to push on. Others can feel sorry for you—take care of you; it's easier, at least it seems so. But what happens when we give up is that we try to find other avenues to make up for what we lost. Often, those avenues are devastatingly more painful than struggling to get what we need to be independent. Giving up our independence, giving up our dream, is like dying. The key is not to give up but to be realistic, to be optimistic, and to find the support one needs. Then, apply the hard work. Though it may take a lifetime, it is time well spent.

I'll never forget one day when I learned for the first time what many people thought of me when I found the courage to disclose. It would be a day that made me certain I had to succeed. The naysayers were out there, and they were beginning to show their colors. It was the day of a required exam; I had to go to the college to take the exam. I had talked with the professor on the telephone; he had received my note from disability services and knew I would take the test outside the class in a quiet area. On my arrival, I waited to talk with him to let him know who I was. I'll never forget his statement to me that day; he looked at me with surprise and said, "You know, you're such an attractive young lady, you really shouldn't let anyone know you have learning disabilities." I wasn't sure if I should laugh, cry, or be angry. I walked out stunned and confused. What did he mean by that statement? Do other people with learning disabilities look different than me? Should I be more ashamed of what I have? Is it so bad to have LD? I couldn't concentrate on that test and consequently did not do very well. I was perseverating the entire time I was taking the test, thinking about the intent of the statement. All of a sudden I felt sick—it occurred to me that others might be thinking this same thing. But I had to disclose or I would fail, just like my first semesters in college out of high school. I had no choice; the decision was simple, but only God knew how painful it would be.

After 2 years, I was out of the community college system. I had completed four semesters and was headed for the 4-year university. My son was ready to begin kindergarten; my daughter would begin staying with a lady in the neighborhood. I had carefully chosen another university to attend. To make my decision, I looked at things such as the disability services department, the number of other students with learning disabilities, the help that would be offered to me, and the size of the classes. This university looked like my best choice. So with help from VR and some guaranteed student loans, I would embark on my future with the great American debt following me. People with learning disabilities need to be aware of the resources available to them; there are so many sources on how to choose colleges, career colleges (a new phrase for vocational/technical schools), or any school for that matter if you have LD or ADHD.

Once I left the community college and began at the university, things began to change for me. I had a better sense of self. Now I was a junior in college. A junior; it was hard to believe. I felt like I was dreaming. I felt like I was watching a movie of someone else who was being successful. How could it be me? I'll never forget the day I got the call from Maggie asking me if I would be interested in teaching a class with her at the community college. The same woman who had inspired me and helped me to shine was still pushing me; she believed in me. I was ecstatic—me, teaching? It was a dream come true! Not only would I get to teach at the college level but also I would get paid. My first real professional job! Of course, I had to share this with everyone, our friends and my family, as well as Paul's family. The only ones who were thrilled for me were Paul and my family. Again, I didn't get the hint; I was going on and on about this great accomplishment but it was no big deal to Paul's family; again they thought I was bragging. The problem was I wasn't satisfied with their reaction. To me, their response, "That's great," with no questions about it meant, "Yeah, okay, fine. Now let's go on to the next subject." With most of them, I was right, that is how they felt; I could tell when they would walk away as I was talking. It's too bad that small accomplishments aren't treated like all success; it shouldn't matter how big or small, it is a beginning to happiness and independence.

Excitement and fear passed over me. I knew I had much to offer, but I was afraid. Maybe the students in the class I was to help teach would be able to see my insecurity, my fear. Would they laugh when I misspelled words on the board, or if they couldn't read my writing? Would I have to read out loud to them? Would I stumble? Would they judge me as harshly or more harshly than others did? My fears turned to anxiety though I never let anyone know just what I was feeling. In doing so, I would only cause more harm. I knew I had to accept the position; I knew it would make a big positive impact on my future as well as help the family income a little. So with inner skepticism, I accepted.

Time went by, and life became more hectic. I began to feel the pressure to graduate as soon as possible. The stress of not having enough income to sustain my full-time status (I was making only a minuscule amount of money from my part-time teaching), child care costs, the mortgage, and all the bills of just living became frightfully cumbersome. Because I had been succeeding in school up to this point and felt I had mastered the fine art of studying, it was time to pick up the pace and carry a fuller load. I started out at 14 hours, then 15 hours, then 18 hours, then 20, and finally it was over, but not without a lot of aggravation, weight loss, hostility, anger, stress, and overall chaos at home.

It was also during this time when my dream of majoring in education ended. Though I had the grades, I couldn't pass an essential education exam required by the state, and at that time, no one seemed to know how to help me. I was devastated. I couldn't understand why, if a person was maintaining a 3.4 grade-point average, an exception or accommodation couldn't be made. I remember a person in the education department telling me that if I couldn't pass these tests without an accommodation I didn't belong in the classroom. I wanted to die; all my dreams were ruined. That day I remember walking down the hall crying, trying not to become hysterical. All I ever wanted was to teach. I wanted to teach high school in behavioral science or social science. I knew I could have done a great job, but it was all over. I never told anyone but my husband about this, just that I was changing majors.

I thought it would be a sign of weakness, and all my successes would amount to nothing.

In addition, my son, though getting by in kindergarten, was still not doing well. His verbal communication skills were very weak; his fine motor and gross motor skills were still a problem. And his behavior was suffering as he was beginning to show his frustration that no one understood him and that he was having trouble understanding others. It was in first grade, however, that my dream that he would no longer have these disabilities was quashed. He hadn't been cured; he just managed while in kindergarten. His first-grade teacher had taught for 30 years, same school, same grade. In front of him one day, while she was holding him by the arm as if to lift him into the air, I remember her saying "In all my years of teaching, I have never seen such a child; he is the class clown." Her eyes were flashing at me. "He is worthless, disrespectful, he's not trying!" My alarm bells went off, my eyes filled with tears, partly out of anger, mostly out of sadness and my own memory. Now my son was living in my world. I looked at Justin and told him to go outside on the swings and wait for me. He complied, looking at me with his big, wide eyes—scared of what would happen next. I winked at him and caught a glimmer of hope in his eyes. With tears streaming down my face and my voice shaking, I then proceeded to tell this teacher that I would not stand there and let her talk about my son that way. I explained to her in strong language that he was a human being and a 6-year-old child and that no one had the right to do that to anyone else. My final words to her were that she had made her bed and now she would have to lie in it, that because she told him he was a class clown he would obey her and become one, and that I would be reporting her to the principal. She looked at me and said, "But your son is so disruptive to the class; he walks across radiators, and one day he called me a big, fat frog face." I looked at her confused, not knowing what to say, and responded, "Can you blame him? What else can he do when someone like you abuses him day after day?" I knew that although his behavior wasn't appropriate, the year before he had not behaved this way, and the reason was that his kindergarten teacher cared. In first grade, he was only reacting in the only way he knew how. My poor baby was suffering the way that I had year after year. I felt helpless; fortunately, my little talk seemed to make her back down, either that or the principal did.

Needless to say, I knew that things were not getting better for him so I had to find an alternative for the following year. The next step was to set up some diagnostic testing to determine my son's eligibility for a private school. (It was through this process as well as through my own experiences and my strengths in understanding the emotional mind that I arrived at the decision to work in the field helping individuals with hidden disabilities.) Fortunately, he qualified and for 3 years he would spend time in a smaller, contained classroom with a loving, understanding, and empathetic teacher who would change his life forever.

Justin's experiences triggered all kinds of emotions in me, as did the loss of my teaching dream. I found myself thinking about death again. I knew I needed help so I sought out a counselor on campus and tried to work through the crushing blows. I knew there had to be options available for me, so I quickly changed my major to psychology, as I had done well in elective classes and really had an interest. I would figure out the rest of it in a relatively quick amount of time; after all, I had to hurry through this. I don't know what kept me going. Counseling certainly helped, but as usual I quickly recovered. I decided that the person was an idiot and that I didn't need her, and I was on my manic way again. It seemed time after time I would get hit with some situation that would rock my world. I wondered if others dealt with these types of things and how they would cope. Was my reaction normal, or did I internalize it differently and take it too hard because I already felt inept? Each time something would go wrong I would find myself blaming it on my own stupidity. I was constantly struggling to find a place in which I would fit and seeking out people who could help me find a way.

Fortunately for me, I had met many very supportive and wonderful professors. They saw how hard I worked, my dedication, my interest, my enthusiasm. Because it was a small university and because I worked hard, I only had a couple of professors question my LD. One I will never forget; I think he learned as much from me as I did from him. He was a professor of philosophy, a real naturalist as well. He owned no car, no television, and had seven children. He rode a bike or walked to school daily. He was a brilliant man, very intimidating, but I liked him. He was funny and his Critical Thinking class consisted of mostly discussion, much to my benefit. Though we had to read articles such as "Why I Am a Total Pacifist" to "Questions of Christianity," he provoked, encouraged, and debated those articles with us. I had no problem with this; I loved it. My strength was in talking, and I had no difficulty in theorizing and solving dilemmas. I was able to listen to him and participate in discussions with other students with no difficulties. But as usual, I disclosed to let him know about my test taking and my reading and sequencing difficulties. About mid-semester, he called me into his office for a talk. I was doing well in his class using all the typical accommodations, written work on tape, untimed tests, and a reader for tests. His opening statement to me was odd, complimentary, and compelling. He told me he had asked to see me because he wanted to tell me I was one of his brightest students; he told me I was doing very well in this class during discussion. He explained that my tests were good and well thought out, but he did feel I needed some help academically. He told me he personally didn't believe learning disabilities existed in people who were in college, that society teaches us to have weaknesses such as these. There was nothing wrong really, he said; it was a learned problem, and one that I bought into.

After having experienced his discussions in class I knew that arguing with him would be futile—I had to convince him with more evidence. He made a compelling point, and I was intrigued. Knowing him like I did, I asked him how he knew these things. He responded with a serious look that it was because I was much too bright to be LD. I asked him why I did poorly in school when I wasn't receiving accommodations, and now I was almost on the dean's list in school. Again, he stated that it was because I didn't believe in myself and my capabilities so I had accepted what seemed right at the time. Then the big shock occurred: He challenged me, stating that he could teach me to read and write. If I was willing to work with him the next semester on a one-to-one basis, he would give me a pass-fail with three credits, but I would have to work for it without accommodations.

The next semester began, and I was given an article. Week after week we would sit; he would read my report on the article, mark it in red pen, and say, "No, this is not it." The professor would show me again what to look for, how to understand it, and how to read it. Finally, toward the end of the semester, I was still working on the same article and still not getting it. I was on the verge of falling apart when all of a sudden out of the blue, I picked up his glasses. When he asked for them, I responded, "You can't read without them, right?"

"Why, of course not," he responded.

"Well, I believe the only difference between you and me is that for you they found a way to accommodate your inability to read the printed word; for me they haven't yet found a way." It was that logic, those simple words that changed our style. From then on he read the article to me, we discussed it, and I passed the course. He later told me that he was once 100% skeptical about me having LD. He still had a hard time understanding it, but he was now a believer. He is certainly not alone in this belief. Many people do not under-stand or even believe in LD, not until it hits close to home; even then it is hard to believe. If people can't see something, they often think it must not be real, but like a diagnosis of cancer, they begin to understand that the unseen can at times be very real. This experience left me thankful to him for taking a risk with me and proud of myself for accepting the challenge. I learned a lot about myself, that I could find a way even when the situation looks hopeless.

Though college was a wonderful experience overall, by this time in my life, I had other issues that were not so pleasant. My relationship with my husband was becoming complicated; his short fuse with my son and his lack of motivation frustrated me. Perhaps what was most difficult was my knowledge that I embarrassed him in social situations. We used to go with some of his friends on weekend trips to one of their farms, a group of eight adults would go to swim, ride horses, and relax. I was still not comfortable with people in a social setting in which I had to be around them for a weekend. I knew I could not sustain a conversation outside of my immediate knowledge base: school and learning disabilities, and I knew from past experiences that this was perceived as bragging or talking about myself too much. So I would go and be nervous the whole time; I would offer to help the women when they were in the kitchen (pretty traditional, unfortunately) but I would get this gut feeling that I was "intruding." One time we (the girls) sat down to play cards; I did not want to, but I remember Paul telling me to make an effort to be friendly, not be "a bitch" like he felt I was behaving. So, I did; the game began. I had to explain that I didn't know the rules of the game, so one of the ladies explained it to me. I felt a heat wave come over me. I didn't understand; it meant that I was going to have to add and remember. I asked her to explain it one more time; she was relatively patient, but the other two were sneering. After one round of the game I quit, finally explaining that I didn't do well with games because I had learning disabilities. You could have heard a pin drop—dead silence. But their nonverbal language said it all: "We always knew something was wrong with you." As I walked out onto the porch with another drink in my hand (a growing problem), I sat down in a corner with tears in my eyes, looking everywhere in sight to find my husband.

When he arrived and asked why I was alone on the porch, I explained that I had tried but I just couldn't do it. I just didn't fit in. He was angry with me, telling me it was my fault entirely and that I needed to grow up. I was an embarrassment to him—if only he knew that I was an embarrassment to myself. Everyone ignored me for the rest of the weekend except for socially appropriate exchanges and pleasantries. I just sank further and further into my drinking and pretended to be drunk, though really I was simply horrified that I even existed.

I would become self-reflective a lot, increasingly so through the years, though even as a child I was always trying to figure things out, having random thought after random thought, idea after idea. Now it was that way when I was up and when I was down; only when I was down, it was intentional criticism after criticism. How stupid you are, how much of a social rube you are, you're ugly, too fat, uninteresting, clumsy, why do you even live? My own mind did more damage to me than I got from anyone in that group.

Like everything in my life, things happened, and I still found a way to move on. Soon, it was time to graduate. It was hard to believe. I was so excited. No one else shared my level of excitement—how could they, after all, it was just a bachelor's degree. But to me it was like a release from prison. Of course, in the world of professional work, I would come across more bars to success. Now that I had completed the degree that took me 4 years (along with many summer and interim sessions), I had to decide on a career focus (although I would not advise any person to wait this late). After much research and counseling interventions, I discovered that I did possess some very interesting, transferable skills. I began to see that my years of public speaking, my four semesters of teaching a life-skills class to young adults with learning disabilities, would prove helpful as I moved into a career that would fulfill, at least in some ways, my desire to teach. The field I found that I was suited for was human resources. Though I had no training or experience in that area, my degree in psychology along with my experience would help me. At one seminar I took, I also discovered that I was gifted in the art of networking. This discovery empowered me. I was experiencing extreme highs at that time; nothing would get in my way.

In matching my skills to those of a human resources professional, I still had much to do before I would even begin my networking to find the perfect job. I spent hours at the library calling or writing for more information on the field. I had to learn to talk the language; I had to know what type of job I could potentially obtain with my limited experience. Through my research, I learned that the easiest position to obtain would be that of a recruiter for entry-level jobs; however, what I was really interested in was being a developmental trainer. I realized that I would have to prove my ability and aptitude in this type of job; I took the grand leap and looked at how I would get there from being a recruiter.

I knew what I needed to do. I could talk to people with more authority on what I could do and find out what I needed help on. It all seemed so simple. This, however, is just one piece that needs to be considered; there is so much more involved in finding a good career fit when one has hidden disabilities. Being realistic about one's goals is critical; so is listening to the experts explain what needs to be done, and taking the advice carefully and analytically. So now that I was armed with information, I could begin networking to find my career.

I was determined that this would happen. I had done the research and knew what I needed to do to get ahead; I realized the barriers, and I was positive about my future. I had all the necessary ingredients for success, or at least some of them. There was one piece I had not cleared up in my head; it looked good on paper, it worked well in college, but I knew from experiences in a social setting that disclosing my learning disability could become a problem if it wasn't handled just right.

I was quickly transformed into the role of fear-stricken person. I found myself developing that feeling of incompetence and anxiety rather quickly. I felt like I was sinking in quicksand. My mind was racing a mile a minute: "How could I explain this in a job interview? They probably don't know anything about it and they wouldn't want anything to do with me anyway. They'd probably see me as a liability." The Americans with Disabilities Act (ADA, PL 101-336) had just been signed and I knew my rights but I didn't want to demand anything. I wanted to be hired for what I could do, what I was capable of, and not focus on what I couldn't do. That should be secondary and only if there was something that needed to be accommodated on the job. I made the decision, however: I had to disclose and take my chances.

I really had no choice—with the severity of my learning disabilities I knew from past experience that if I took a job, they would eventually show up. I thought it best to be honest. By the time I had graduated, I had learned new coping strategies, but I was still only reading at about the fifth-grade level. My math skills were still only that of a third grader, and my overall memory-recall ability was a serious concern. But how could I disclose and still maintain a positive, professional, and credible attitude? I decided I must go forward with the networking; that would be my tool to determine how to disclose. It was safe, and I knew people would feel more comfortable being honest with me. Networking is really a useful tool for all people but mostly for people with disabilities. We need whatever edge we can have to "get ahead of the crowd." In networking you begin with a goal such as the one I had, to determine if this is the field for you.

Building the network was no easy task. The day after my final exam, I set up my office at home. I spent 40 hours a week looking for a job, and with balancing family duties and my own fears, it was an exhausting process. I kept myself going by setting a regular schedule just like a work week. My days went like this: up at 6:00 A.M., take the kids to day care 3 days a week, work around them the other 2 days, end around 11:00 P.M. Some days were better than others. I remember the frustration of going over those daily personalized cover letters written by the dozen, correcting them with endless effort, making certain nothing was wrong, and just as I would think it was perfect, there was yet another imperfection. It was frustrating; I ached for some sense of security, some stability. Though everyone goes through the pains of looking for work, for me, in my mind anyway, I was incompetent. Even though I had earned a degree, I was not as capable as was the next person. How and why would anyone want to hire me? No one knew this feeling, not even my husband. When I tried to tell him, he just told me I was being ridiculous, that I was very capable. What he didn't realize, as most people don't, is that when you are dealing with a person who analyzes everything, you are doing nothing more than talking to a wall. Perhaps if he had acknowledged this feeling, then maybe I would have felt validated.

I remember getting the call for my first formal interview for a real opening. I was a nervous wreck. The interview was at a large bank and the position was for a recruiter of nonexempt staff. That meant the person in this position would be responsible for the hiring of mostly clerical-type workers. It was perfect. I eventually interviewed with seven people at the bank. I knew I was in the top three applicants being considered, and while I waited to hear back from the recruiter, I decided that I had to take a risk; I would draft three thank-you letters and hand deliver them. Upon my arrival, the recruiter who interviewed me came out of her office. She was surprised to see me; she asked me to come into her office. That day was one I will never forget: I had disclosed to this company and I was expecting the worst, the common courtesy of rejection. But instead, I got something different. She explained that they had offered the job to another person but he had turned it down. I was next in line, and she was just getting ready to call me. I couldn't believe it. They offered me a nice beginning salary with great benefits and my very own office! I was in heaven.

It was so wonderful; I had a professional job, me, me! I couldn't believe this was happening! I was so excited, but most of all I was scared. Would my LD show up on the job in a negative way? The first day I was shown my beautiful private office: It was huge and had a window. How could this be happening to me? It all seemed like a blur. I had explained to them how I needed to be trained, and they teamed me up with two women who were friendly, open, caring, and responsive. I now know that it was this match that probably created the right type of learning environment. Actually, all of it was right. People were friendly yet professional. They were helpful yet not patronizing; they trusted me right off the bat, they did not enter into the new relationship with skepticism and fear. All the criteria for anyone to be successful existed.

The people who trained me were great, also. They were interested in helping me be successful and listened with great enthusiasm when I explained how I learned and what I needed to enhance my learning. One woman volunteered to read to me whenever I needed her to. Of course, I assured her that that would not be needed often; if I could get the materials well in advance, then I would accommodate myself by working extra hours. And work I did. I would get to work by 7:00 A.M. and not leave until 5:00 or 6:00 P.M., always taking work home with me. The job was great for me; it emphasized all of my skills. It was structured enough for me to stay organized in the system I had developed; it was flexible enough so that I did not get bored, and the departments I was responsible for were wonderful to work with. I was doing so well in my job that by the sixth month I was writing and delivering many training programs in addition to recruitment. Those programs were very well received. Just as I had hoped, the pieces were all falling into place.

During this time, I had also begun my master's program in human resources at the same university. I was burning the candle at both ends. Carrying 6 hours a semester, working 50 hours a week, and doing the domestic stuff was quite taxing. I am sure I was exhausted, but I had a goal and I was going to achieve it. So, I survived on 5 hours of sleep a night, spent my weekends playing catch-up with the family responsibilities, and in any extra time I had I squeezed in some studying. It was fortunate for me that I had wonderful professors, and the coursework was something I could understand. It just made sense to me! I was using my natural talents.

As time moved on, things began to change. The bank was facing problems financially, and there was much concern about our stability. A friend and colleague warned me that because I was hired last I would probably be the first to go. I remember feeling horrified. My dream job was in jeopardy. All I could think of was "here we go again, another crisis," but the president of our department said I was his star employee, how could they let me go? I cried for days. I developed feelings of inadequacy and searched my mind for any mistake I may have made that could have caused me to be at risk. My performance review was a 4.8 out of a 5.0. I was worried that perhaps I had a false sense of security and began to develop a little paranoia. I didn't want to, but I began to look for another job to secure my future. I am sure the kind president of the company was wondering what I was up to. Soon he was not as friendly, not as warm as he once was, and he became aloof. But I swore to my colleague that I would not let anyone know what she had told me.

Two weeks into my search, I interviewed for a job with a very large international company and was offered a position as a recruiter with an $8,000 per year increase and much better benefits. I was excited. My colleague was stunned! As I told everyone that I would be leaving, some things became clear to me that I had not noticed before. It would be my first major lesson in company politics. I had been deceived, for what reason I am not sure. I learned that my job was not in jeopardy and that I should have gone to the president to discuss this concern. Looking back now, I wonder what my colleague's intentions were in telling me my job was in jeopardy. Did she not like me? Was she threatened by me? Was she jealous of my ability to balance so much and still have learning disabilities? Was I an annoyance to her and she just wanted me to go away? Whatever it was, it struck an interesting chord in my mind and heart. I began to develop a sense of cynicism; things aren't always what they seem. Maybe my being too open, too honest, too energetic, scared some people. Though I learned of this, I still decided to leave; after all, thousands of dollars more per year and 100% tuition reimbursement so that I could finish my master's degree was a dream come true! I also began to realize that my LD and ADHD were affecting me more than just academically; they were also entering into the social as well as political corporate climates. In other words, saying the wrong thing to the wrong person at the wrong time (trusting too much because I wanted to be liked and trusted) created a negative impact.

The day I began the new job, I got this incredible sense of fear that crept up like a slow-growing cancer. I didn't feel comfortable; something just didn't seem right. Part of the problem was that I was working in a cubicle; this was a nightmare for me. Though I had requested an office, it would be several months before one could be constructed. I developed a nice working relationship with my boss and a co-worker, and we worked well together, but there were little things that happened that made me feel less than adequate. It wasn't that my boss was doing anything wrong. Actually, she treated everyone this way, but it was as if I had traveled back in time to grade school. I was made to feel less than capable; she used a red pen to mark up everything I did, and we had long discussions in a sort of patronizing way about how I did things. The only consolation I had was that she was consistent in the way she treated everyone; to her, everyone was incompetent. She had sort of a narcissistic personality. I also learned that she hired me because she "wanted to give me a chance." I learned from people in the disability community whom I worked closely with that she felt sorry for me; she thought I was nice and wanted to help me out. Although I appreciated this gesture, honestly, this information aggravated me; it made me feel so stupid. I didn't want this job because I was pitied; I wanted it because I did a good job, because I was qualified, because I met the requirements of the job. I was a token learning disabled person in her eyes.

During the first year of my employment, I was very busy with work, putting in an average of 10 hours per day, not counting lunches. Then 2 nights a week I would go to graduate school for 4 hours at a time. As time went on in my professional career, I developed an incredibly positive reputation from people in the company. Statements and letters to my boss were flowing in; I was complimented for being honest, hardworking, credible, talented, and motivated. Before I knew it, my dreams were coming true, and I was promoted into management. I had a new boss who was wonderful to me, and the department was changing for the better. By the time this had happened, I had finished my master's degree. All the hard work was paying off. I had several wonderful people in the department who helped me with the required reading, kept me organized, and made me feel wonderful. I also had several key directors outside the department who really trusted me. I was on cloud nine again! It was a good thing my education was finished because my work hours increased from 50 hours a week to 60 hours minimum. I had already received two increases and was making close to $40,000 a year with benefits, not bad for someone who had once been told she'd never make it through college.

I began to believe that it was true: Hard work, perseverance, enthusiasm, and honesty would take me down the right path. Unfortunately, good things don't always last. A change in management, a decision that I was not valuable by new management, sent my dream in another direction. Some of my supports changed, some of my job tasks were removed. So, I tried to do things without the benefit of calling people for clarification on written materials and went to meetings cold with written materials that had been given to me at the last moment. I didn't want to rock the boat. Things got harder and harder for me. I couldn't keep up without the supports, and I was feeling like I would sink any minute.

Before I knew it, I was severely depressed, like the switch of a light; late one night I was "talked to" by my boss; actually I was yelled at. I had been told I was not in charge anymore and that my job was changing. I left crushed. It wasn't about my past performance; it had all happened so quickly inside of a month. There were no missed deadlines, no issues with how work was being performed; I made up for the onset of depression by working more hours and taking more notes, and I didn't sleep at all. I was having more difficulties with focusing and remembering, however. I knew I couldn't keep up my performance; it couldn't go on forever; my ability to function was so impaired that I was thinking of only one thing—death.

As I drove home that night, tears streaming down my face, I decided I wanted to die. I was worthless, I was humiliated; it was like being in school again, only now I had proven myself, but it was being taken away. I saw a diesel truck coming behind me on the highway. It was late and dark; I started to turn my small car under the truck, and then quickly I jerked the wheel back as an image of my kids flashed in front of my eyes. I knew I had to do something, get help, and resign from my position. If I didn't, I would likely take my life.

When I told my husband I couldn't go back, he couldn't understand why I was doing this. I was making so much money, couldn't I find something else in the company? he asked. I just couldn't; I was so very depressed, I could barely even function. Finally, he agreed, and I resigned. I began therapy to help me figure out what to do next. After a couple of months of intense therapy, I began to realize that I could not return to the corporate world. I had become gun shy—if it happened again, I would not be able to recover. I also learned that I had bipolar disorder, which explained my depression that had occurred not once but on three major occasions in my life that I knew of for sure, along with serious lengths of time described as mania. I was placed on medications to counterbalance the depression and to control manic episodes.

After a month, I was feeling very good, the calmest I had ever been in my life. So, I began to strategize. I knew I wanted to write a book, I had teaching experience, and I was a dynamite networker. I would start my own business. I would work with people like myself; guide them; train them on how to become independent, on how to find the right training and the right career, on how to advocate for themselves, and on how to know when to disclose or not disclose.

When I announced my decision to my husband, he thought it was okay, but that I was wasting my knowledge and a potentially good income to do something that was very risky. Still he agreed, and I was thankful for that trust. His family was not so supportive, however. It was like I had failed again, and I felt that I was perceived as a flake, someone who was taking advantage of their son. It didn't matter that I was simply trying to survive; I couldn't let them know that; I would have never shared with them how much I wanted to die.

I started the business, and within the first month I had two clients. It wasn't that hard really. In a way you could say I did it all wrong; I just printed business cards, drafted some flyers with help from a woman I knew through an organization I did volunteer work for, and purchased some software, all on the great American debt card. Everything I did was out of common sense; my networking skills brought in my first clients; I didn't need a marketing budget, and I just made calls and followed up. I set it up in my home in the extra room, and before I knew it, I was in business!

Of course, I hadn't thought of things like accounting; I'd just worry about that when I needed to. I also decided that I didn't need medication anymore, I was fine. I didn't have this "bipolar thing," I was just down. I'd be fine. I began shifting my attention to work and relationships. It was interesting in looking back now how much energy I gave to this relationship with my husband's family. I did feel guilt; I had been married to their nephew (Paul's cousin Kyle) — why would I really be accepted? Now, of course, I know why. First, because I married Paul at such a young age, when I was only at 23, and I had already gone through so much trauma, I ignored what I instinctively knew was a serious problem. Second, I needed them so desperately; I had few friends in all these years. I didn't know how to sustain a friendship with women; it was always easy with men, so the friends I did have tended to be men. I believed I could get their attention because I was — in their minds — a possible conquest.

Another issue is hard to discuss, too painful. And it is only fair to state that the reason for this is not owned only by those people I knew; a lot of it was due to me. I didn't know how to engage in conversation in a light manner; I didn't know how to be me, I didn't know how to have fun. I was so serious most of the time; it was how I survived. Some people think being a child and having disabilities is difficult, and it is, but being an adult with hidden disabilities is far worse. It is easier when one is a child because you are not expected to be "perfect." Of course, neither are adults, but in many ways you are expected to carry certain abilities, strengths, interests, or some knowledge of current events so that you can strike up a conversation at a party without the courage of a little glass of wine. For me, this is an area that had become very problematic. When you have so much trouble reading that even a short article in the paper creates frustration, it's hard to have what people consider safe conversations discussing current events or other popular topics. Or, when it is difficult processing information at a party because of all of the external stimuli, people think you are aloof or rude. For me, avoiding some parties was a blessing, but most of the time I really wanted to be there; it meant I was normal, not an outcast, never mind the invitation always came from my husband's friends; I had none of my own.

It seemed like everything I was doing was going wrong; I was getting my business going; it was actually doing really well for a start-up practice. I even got to write a column in a small newspaper focusing on disability issues. But I was lonely; I missed having interaction with people. So, I sought a closer relationship with family. I decided to do what was the worst thing I could do—talk about my practice.

Once, in an attempt to answer one relative's question, it was evident to me that I was perceived as a joke. She said something to me like, "It doesn't seem fair that you and people like you get let off the hook by having untimed tests or oral testing, while the rest of us have to struggle through it." I calmly explained to her that the only difference is we get a little extra time to process, and there is no research that says the untimed tests prove less or more knowledge than timed tests. Being untimed is only for the purpose of time management unless it involves an actual work demonstration that is task related. As far as oral testing, I asked her if she had ever been tested one-to-one, face-to-face with an instructor? I encouraged her to try it sometime and to let me know if she still thinks we are really getting the better deal.

I felt so horrible after that; I couldn't believe that after all that hard work, people still did not believe me. After all, she knew all the late evenings I studied. She knew I worked 60-hour weeks and practically exhausted myself trying to be a full-time mother. Why is it that unless things are done in a way that someone is comfortable with or familiar with, it must not be right? A brain lock exists in so many people; if they looked in the mirror, they probably could remember a time when they had to have something presented differently to them. Unless you do it in the traditional way it doesn't count, at least not in the eyes of some. And that's what I had to remember, only in the eyes of some.

Having learning disabilities as an adult is not so much a problem of the disabilities themselves as it is feeling insecure so much of the time. Perhaps I feel this way because I know my limitations and I have, in the past, unnecessarily increased the difficulties I had. This was due to my insecurity, my need to fit in, and my need to in some way defend my methods when I, myself, felt that I was still cheating at the time—even though logically I knew I was not.

It was these types of situations, or just being ignored in general, that created serious conflict between my husband and me. He just couldn't understand. I used to cry endlessly to myself, drink heavily when I was around certain groups, and have horrible arguments with my husband. He would grow angry at my feelings of frustration and insecurity and compare me to people who were in my eyes not a far cry from being socially inept. Eventually, I would realize, "It's okay, I am who I am, and I do not need to fit in with everyone. Not everyone will like me or understand me. I will find my own way and my own friends."

In the interim, however, doing things by myself or with my kids was the answer. Ironically, one day when I was feeling very rejected I went to a museum. In the past, museums frustrated me because I could not read the information under each item, but there was an exhibit that looked interesting so I chose to attend. On arrival, I noticed the option to wear headphones that would guide people through the exhibit. I figured, why not? In the past, I would have felt too awkward to ask for headphones. When I put them on I followed the verbal instructions. Three hours later, there were tears streaming down my face. For once I had really gotten the full impact of this wonderful exhibit; I had found a way to learn history that I enjoyed, that I understood. I could share my knowledge in conversation; my God, I understood. My inner voices helped me. I was reframing my mind: Yes, I had many hidden disabilities, but I was reminded again of the successes I had had in college using accommodations; I was capable of learning. I had temporarily forgotten this important lesson after being broken down in the corporate world.

I believe that things happen for a reason, and it was at this time in my life that I met a person who would change the way I viewed men forever: Dr. Larry Silver, a clinical psychiatrist whose commentary closes out each chapter of this book. I'll never forget how we met; he was presenting a program in town on learning disabilities and ADHD while I was visiting my parents. At the last minute, I decided to go. I watched, listened, and internalized what he said; it all made sense to me. Dr. Silver was a sincere and genuine man; anyone could tell that. His heart was in his work; he wasn't in it only as a career, but because he lived and breathed it every day. Somehow, I knew we would get along, so during the brown-bag lunch, I was invited by one of my mother's friends to sit at the table with Dr. Silver. As the eight of us sat and talked, we asked questions of Dr. Silver. Eventually, he looked across the table at me, noticed my hyperactive movements, and tossed an orange to me. I caught it and smiled. He asked me if I would like to take a quick walk before the session began again. I was honored and surprised that he asked me to take a walk. During the short 10 minutes we spent talking about why I was at the conference, we formed a bond, one that I knew would continue. His inspiration, words of encouragement, and sincerity would give me hope when things would get rough in the times to come.

Surprisingly, that day I was asked to be interviewed by a local news station because I had graduated from high school there and had done a lot of public speaking. One of the women who was there pulled me out of the presentation to be interviewed. Dr. Silver would also be interviewed. That day turned out to be one that changed my life forever; it was a sign that I had done the right thing, quitting my job and pursuing a career in helping others like myself.

There were other things that were happening in my life, precipitated partially by age and experience, and the growing realization that I felt that my husband didn't love me. Though this meant terrible sadness for me, in some ways it forced me to see my children and myself differently. Tess, my little girl who is like a clone of myself, had been exhibiting signs since she was very young that she had learning disabilities also, but because she was holding her own at the time I would just wait and watch. I saw in her a strong spirit; she was very busy; beautiful; and talented musically, artistically, and kinesthetically. People loved to be around Tess; she was outgoing and had very strong interpersonal skills. It was Tess who was able to show me the most compassion when I was feeling "different." There was a time when she was only 8 years old and we were waiting in a hair salon; she was reading on her own until she came across a word she couldn't make out. She asked me to read it to her; I could not make it out either. She said, "It's okay, Mommy, I understand why you can't read it; it's 'cause you have dyslexia. I love you." This was so profound a statement from a child. I didn't share with her that feeling of sadness, disappointment, and embarrassment I felt. I held it in; there was no need to talk about it, and somehow I knew she understood. There was another time I couldn't help her with her math homework. Again, she understood. I remember looking in her eyes with a sense of sadness; it was as if she could read my thoughts. It must be hard to be a child of a mother who cannot help with certain types of work at the third-grade level. I love her so much; when I think of how she has had to learn so much so young, I imagine how this can help her or hurt her. She is the nurturer in the family when I am not around; when her big brother is hurting, she goes to him, talks to him, and shares with me her understanding of his problem. We talk often about our feelings. I am sure she will be a very secure, understanding, and bright adult, and who knows? Maybe she'll become a person who can solve some of the mystery of these disabilities.

Tess's ability to see that her mom has flaws and that it is okay allowed me to look at my son in a very different way. His frustration with language was severe, and consequently this put him in many sad situations. As a mother, I watched him try to figure out how to fit in; he was clumsy, so sports were out; he was preoccupied with objects, so other kids found him "weird." But he didn't have mental retardation as they had once thought; he was diagnosed instead as having learning, attention, and language disabilities, and the autistic tendencies still applied. He knew how others saw him at school, however; he would scream out of frustration "I'm so stupid." He conjured it up in his mind just like I did, and I would argue that while it is all internal perception, it is perception based on reactions from others. He wasn't like the other kids and he knew it. What he didn't know was that in the not-too-distant future, these differences would be a blessing for him. He would come into his own, and I would be able to tell thousands of people how proud I am of this young man who was given such a negative future.

I always tell my kids that we all face challenges in life, and it is important to remember that no matter where we go in life, no matter what we do, we will encounter events that will change the way we think and feel. It is when we give up trying to understand how we think and feel, or trying to find new methods of making things work for us and others, that we are defeated. Just when you think you have no one, remember—you have yourself.

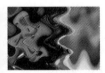

INSIGHTS AND INTERVENTIONS
by Larry B. Silver, M.D.

Veronica moved into her young adult years carrying all of the emotional baggage of her childhood and adolescence. She was full of self-doubt and had a poor self-image. She continued to believe that she was dumb, incompetent, and inadequate. What else could she have felt after a lifetime of reinforcement that these feeling were true? The problem is that when one's inner world cannot provide comfort or reassurance that one is a good person, one must look for this reassurance from the outside world. This dependency on external feedback to feel good about one's self leaves an individual vulnerable. Any look, comment, or criticism confirms one's internal beliefs and can make one feel inadequate, often depressed. Any positive feedback is appreciated but doubted. "If he really knew how dumb or bad I am, he would not think or say that." This person is not only vulnerable to anyone in his or her outside word; the outside world constantly confirms his or her worst fears. It is a self-fulfilling action.

The other price one pays for feeling so negative and bad inside is that he or she seeks others who confirm these feelings. He or she is uncomfortable with praise or positive interactions. The person doesn't trust that others are sincere. "How could she believe this? Wait until she gets to know the real me." So, Veronica, like so many other Veronicas in the world, is most comfortable with people who are critical and abusive. These relationships are in harmony with her inside world. She is constantly critical and abusive of herself. If Veronica were a patient of mine, I would have worked to help her understand and accept herself. Until she could make peace with her inside world and learn to love herself, she would be sentenced to a lifetime of moving in and out of destructive relationships. There would be no inner peace. She would be depressed. Unfortunately, such help was not available to her until much later in her life.

Veronica started college. This time, her learning disabilities were known. She received support services and accommodations. She worked with a wonderful counselor, Maggie, who helped her understand her disabilities and *how* to learn. Maggie was the start of Veronica's future. She was a crucial person in her life. For the first time, someone Veronica trusted held a mirror and showed her that she was not dumb or incompetent but instead had great potential. Maggie showed Veronica that she had to learn about her disabilities and discover how to master them rather than have them defeat her.

Veronica's son, Justin, became another mirror in her life. She believed that he had her genes and her brain. He struggled in school as she did. His teachers misunderstood him and treated him as she had been treated at his age. At first, she looked into the mirror and saw herself. She hated herself and was angry with herself. She began to get angry with Justin. He reinforced her own feelings of inadequacy. He made her feel guilty for giving him this curse.

Fortunately for both of them, she understood what she was doing and stopped. She knew that she did not want him to experience what she had experienced. She offered unconditional love. She became his advocate. She would not ever allow teachers to do to him what had been done to her. This was another turning point in her life. In my practice, I meet other parents with learning disabilities who have children with the same disabilities. They look into the mirror and get angry. Some are never able to empathize by remembering what they felt like as a child. This would be too painful. They continue to attack. They do not become advocates. The child pays a dear price for this.

As Veronica moved from community college to college to the world of work, she took her poor self-image and low self-esteem with her. She continued to question or reject any positive feedback and to seek out relationships that reinforced her internal beliefs. She continued to feel inadequate and bad. She continued to be vulnerable and to find people who confirmed her own beliefs.

It is possible that Veronica had been moving in and out of depression all of her life and that this depression was not totally a result of her internal conflict. In her mid-20s (and in retrospect, much earlier), she began to experience periods of what is called *hypomanic* behavior. This means she would have ideas and feelings of grandiosity. She would become very active and her mind would race. Her thoughts would be so active that she could not stop to relax or to sleep. During these periods, she could become increasingly angry, if not enraged. She was diagnosed with bipolar disorder (formerly called manic depressive disorder). We now know that there is a high frequency of relationship between learning disabilities, attention-deficit/hyperactivity disorder, bipolar disorder, and other disorders. Chapter 10 explains this in greater detail.

7

THE PROMISED LAND

GROWING MATURITY

A woman came up to me,
held my hand clasped in
hers, and said with
tears in her eyes,
"Now I understand
what my child has been
going through all
these years."

T hings don't always work out as one plans. Several years went by as I worked very hard to build my disabilities consulting business, draft a rough copy of a book, and try to hold on to my marriage. The next few years, I would discover that my dream of a happy marriage was gone; I believed that the man I loved was actually happier when I was away. And if that wasn't enough, my business was experiencing serious growing pains. It started out simply enough; I had a concept of helping people like myself find hope and meaning in their lives while teaching others what it is like to have hidden disabilities. For so many, learning disabilities are seen as affecting only the academic areas. I had to help people understand that having difficulties academically is just one aspect of learning disabilities. If you can't read, write, do math, process information, sequence, organize, synthesize, and read nonverbal cues, to name a few, problems will naturally occur in other areas. Somehow I had to find a way to let people know that these hidden disabilities are lifelong disabilities; and if ignored, they can lead to lifelong disaster. I don't think many banks would have given me a loan with that mission alone, but I wasn't looking for one. I started with virtually nothing, knowing it was a risk, and I have kept that focus all along.

Today, I can see the results: The work is emotionally and spiritually rewarding, and I'm not starving! Those results, however, did not occur without a lot of hard work, introspection, and some relapses into negative ways of thinking accompanied by lots of tears, loss, and soul searching. These experiences were an awakening to me. Although many of them were devastating, I have found a way to go on. The awareness of the types of mistakes we so often make when we have a sense of insecurity or uncertainty often allows us tremendous insights. Only through experience and education can we really provide the best help to others; only through trials and tribulations can we begin to look deeply enough to put the pieces together and build our own success. So I pushed on, taking more risks and learning more truths, but this is life, and it isn't an easy path. When you add growing up feeling inadequate on top of life's daily lessons, sometimes it takes a bit longer to figure things out.

Though painful, starting my own business was without a doubt the best thing that could have ever occurred. In the past, when asked by people in the field, even family, "Why do you feel stupid?" the only explanation I could give was, "It is just how I feel." It was only after building up this business and from reflecting on all that I have learned in the 4 years prior to publishing this book that it all began to fit. I have learned which pieces have been missing not only in my life but also in the lives of so many people with hidden disabilities.

At this time in my life, still a young adult but married with two children, I would reflect on my feeling that I wasn't successful in academics and that I had to work so hard at everything I did. I believed that I wasn't very good at many things, especially without accommodations or a tremendous amount of help. But it was really more than that, and throughout this chapter, you will begin to see just how easy it is to slip into this negative thought pattern when you struggle to remember, process, understand, or stay in a consistently calm mood. No matter how much you have achieved, often it makes no difference—no one can tell you except *you* how very wonderful things can be. But with that, you will also learn how very normal these feelings are and how to help yourself or someone you love work through the pain.

The energy I had when I decided to start this business was very strong. I had experienced this type of realistic and natural energy a time or two before, in college, getting that first job at the bank, feeling like I could take on the world. I was like a kid who had just learned to ride a bike and was experiencing the freedom and power, but at the same time I was just fearful enough to watch out. I became dependent on too many people's opinions instead of trusting myself. That old insecurity was creeping in, and I was terrified that I wouldn't make it.

It all started out with a bang. My first month of business I brought in several seminars, and I was networking all over the city.

Some of the programs I was delivering were received so well that they led to more and more. I was elected a board member to a very well-respected association that serves those with learning disabilities. Furthermore, I was made a commissioner on a local city program specializing in disability issues. My hopes were rising; I was getting some recognition and I felt confident that things were going to work. I began to purchase materials to enhance my business, and then I began to develop more materials for program delivery, including brochures and business cards. I was excited and nervous. I wasn't sure how or where to start so I just started, right in the midst of cognitive chaos. I had big dreams like most new business owners; I wanted to make a difference and I was determined to do it. I had something special to offer. Little did I know that this beginning would require more than just sheer determination. I would learn whom my supporters—and my enemies—were.

Things soon became more and more confusing. I had to remind myself to look at my experience, all the training I had done, and the fact that I had gotten national and local speaking engagements. I had also previously done a lot of volunteer work with many groups, offered my time, my enthusiasm, and my dedication. This work was done both prior to and during the time my business was up and running. This involvement was critical for me, not for my business as much as for my sanity. I needed to be around people—people who I felt cared about me. What I didn't realize again was that this was business, and most people, even those who profess to be in it for the common good, are in it for themselves. I chose to ignore my gut feeling that perhaps I couldn't trust certain people. I was lonely and desperate.

I found that working alone created a lot of problems for me; I was greatly in need of the social aspects that my previous experiences with school and work had provided me. I needed the company of people with whom I could talk, share, and feel a part of something important. When I did find those relationships, however,

I began to notice nonverbal behaviors from some people that at certain times indicated I was just being tolerated, leaned on only when something was needed. I couldn't understand how, when I was receiving thousands of evaluations stating that I had delivered an excellent program, it was still so hard to feel that I fit in. I still was having trouble finding groups of people who were in the field for the same reason I was. Weren't we all there to help spread the word? Soon I would learn that just like the corporate business world, even in the field of disability-related issues there would be people who were in it for their own personal gain, unwilling to see the big picture.

I'll never forget one occasion after the start of my business when I was asked to introduce three speakers at a national conference. I was honored because of the prestige of this particular organization. I worked very hard to memorize the names on the sheet I had been given, but one name was particularly hard so in advance I asked the man to please pronounce his name. He did, and I wrote it as he said it so that I could create my own phonetic cue. I thought I had it but during the introduction, I said his name incorrectly anyway. I felt so bad. After the session when I was collecting the evaluations I found one that read ". . .so unprofessional, she couldn't pronounce the speaker's name properly." It sent me in a tailspin. I was crushed. Maybe most of the world would blow this off, but I was so down I wanted to die. It took all I had to disappear from the program only to cry in my car, saying to myself "You're so dumb!" I couldn't even get a name right. In my mind it wasn't unlike what happened to the main character in the Stephen King novel *Carrie*. She thought the whole school was laughing at her when the pig's blood fell on her head at the prom, when in reality it was only a couple of people. It might have only been this one person who thought that I looked like an idiot, but to me it was the whole world.

I don't think people realize how one comment like that can create so much pain. It was a human error; I hadn't shared inaccurate information, I hadn't misled anyone, and no one was hurt. All, that is, except for me. I wonder if it gave that person a good feeling to negatively critique someone on such an insignificant issue? Wouldn't it have been better to approach me and ask me a question that would have been helpful and supportive? We never know what is going on with people; it would be so nice if we could all try to consider that maybe the person is experiencing some difficulties and offer guidance or help, or just not waste everyone's time if the issue is not critical.

Though I knew I was good at what I did and my clients and their families believed that I was a miracle worker, it didn't make any difference that I was viewed this way. Instead, I quickly shifted to blaming these types of occurrences and the problems I had in general with working for myself on my learning disabilities and all of the traumas I had experienced. After all, in my mind when I was sinking into sadness and depression it didn't matter; if I weren't so stupid, then I wouldn't have these types of lifelong problems. It was too bad that I didn't believe in myself. Soon I began to perseverate. Things began to slip; the big bang at the beginning of the company was slowing down and I thought it was because of my own inability to run a business. It was as if I had slipped back several years and was losing so much of the confidence I had acquired. It seemed everything was going wrong: not enough clients, not enough speaking engagements, endless letters and calls in which nothing really seemed to occur. I had some business, enough to keep going, but I became overwhelmed. Things like billing, invoicing, tracking leads, making purchases for the business, and reading to keep up on the latest research and trends were difficult. I was all alone and I was scared; I desperately needed some support, but it seemed that wherever I turned it would come back to hit me in the face.

After hours of work and time I began to learn, through people who *did* know my work and my abilities, that I was not being taken seriously. People believed that I had a hidden agenda. Although this information was given to me secondhand, I began to learn about comments people were making about my inability to do the work because I was LD. Some stabbed me in the back, others stole information I had created and discounted me, which led to much distress in my life. That information brought back painful memories.

The one blessing I had through all of this was a new friend, Jim. He was like the big brother I had always needed. There was never anything sexual between Jim and me, but we had a closeness that no one could really understand. I am sure our colleagues talked about us. His strength and our openness allowed both of us to finally find in each other a true friend. We both knew that no matter what we shared we would not laugh at, think less of, or reject each other. Jim, who had much more education than I had, also had learning disabilities. Together, through long serious discussions and gentle teasing, we decided that we would always have to work much harder than the average person does; it was simply a fact. And more important, we realized that good deeds in this world aren't always well received. Together, however, we could help each other get through this cause. We knew we could trust each other.

It was at this time I was also conversing with a company in Arizona. They had asked me to do some work for them, and they were pleased with the results. I had met the president of this company, Rob, a handsome man who made me very nervous, on a committee out of state a year or so prior to this. He was bright, articulate, and, in my opinion, very arrogant. I wasn't sure if I could trust him, but after being around him a couple of times at different conferences where he asked nothing of me, he won my trust. I rated him up there with Jim and Larry Silver in terms of how much I admired and respected him for his intelligence, and that is a selective group to be compared with.

Rob, I later learned, also was skeptical of me. I decided, however, that someone of his experience could offer good advice, and although I didn't want to hear it all the time, it was he who explained to me what type of things I may encounter. In fact, he told me that this field was difficult in that there were a lot of naysayers, a lot of skeptics of adults with learning disabilities. Though at first I didn't listen, deep down I knew that he was right. I guess I was always a little naive, trusting people too much, believing that if I had a genuine desire and commitment people would appreciate it. I didn't want people to see me in a controversial way, but now I was beginning to understand.

I was running my own business as a for-profit in a traditionally not-for-profit field. People were seeing me as a moneygrubber, someone who wanted to use the field for my own benefit. What they didn't know was that the single reason that I operated a for-profit business was because I didn't understand nonprofit, and frankly, it looked too complicated for me to handle. Instead, I found out from Jim and Rob that I had to be careful because people would comment on how attractive and flirtatious I was, that it would be perceived that I was after something. They discussed how comments from many men would be focused on my friendliness, my outgoing nature and appeal and how many women would comment on my being too flirtatious, that I was "up to something." I never realized before how this type of friendliness could be perceived as negative. I was just being me; I wasn't being anyone who was trying to cause harm or who had hidden intentions. I had always been like this; it was how I survived. But now it was backfiring. I guess what hurt most is that the naysayers didn't even know me; they only knew of me from the mouths of those who didn't know me either. They didn't know a thing about my education, my experience, and my abilities. They never did ask me questions about my thoughts or ideas. They just assumed. The real world was upon me, and I wasn't prepared. I thought I had seen it all, but I still had more to learn. Now it was time to take a good, hard look at who I was, what I needed to do, and whom I could trust. But before that would happen, I would experience a lot of turmoil.

I'll never forget working with a professional in the field, a physician, who criticized me for misspelling someone's last name. This physician actually called me on the phone and yelled. He was telling me that I was incompetent and stupid. I couldn't understand his rationale; it wasn't even a public letter, and it was directed to one person who really wouldn't have cared if his name was spelled wrong. It was so upsetting to me, that one person could hurt me so much. Why did I care, he was the one being ridiculous; but the point was that I did care and it hurt me a lot—so much so I began to doubt my own abilities again. Maybe I couldn't help anyone, maybe I should just go back to the human resources field and play it safe; people in the business world liked me or at least respected me; my assertiveness and hard work were appreciated.

I felt like I had gone through the wringer. Things were chaotic. I wasn't making the money I needed to; I knew I could get a job back in human resources for a lot more money and stop people's questioning of why I was doing this, and in that field I could succeed. But something was about to change all of that. It was at that time that I presented at yet another conference and all the pieces began to fall together. At that conference, I heard a statement I had gotten so many times before, but this time it was like words from heaven—as if an angel had been sent to touch my soul. A woman came up to me, held my hand clasped in hers, and said with tears in her eyes, "I've heard many presentations on learning disabilities, but until today, I really didn't understand. Now I understand what my child has been going through all these years. You have given me a reason to believe. Thank you; please keep helping others." I felt surges of power come over me, I felt this endless flow of happiness, and I was on cloud nine. I knew then that I had to continue, no matter what it took. I couldn't let others suffer as much as I had and so many of us have if I could provide even the slightest hope for a few.

I began to remember other comments, things that struck me as being so meaningful. People would thank me for giving them hope; they would call me, send me letters of support and encouragement. I had professionals tell me that they had never had anyone present on the realities of being learning disabled like I had; it all made sense to them now. Upon my return home, I dug up all my prior evaluations and found the comments were similar. People were pleased with what I had to say; I had provided information, hope, understanding, and a message of belief. I cried to myself knowing what I had to do; I just needed to find a way. I had to shake this insecurity. I had to find people I could trust; I would flounder and fall some more but I would not give up.

I needed something; I thought my life was falling apart. All the energy I had in the beginning was growing dim; I didn't know what else to do to make things better, and I didn't know what to do to get my husband's attention. Ironically, Rob called me about that time. He asked me to come out and do some consulting. I was honored. During the time of my visit I became familiar with his program, The Life Development Institute, and admired the very realistic approach they used to help individuals with LD and ADHD become independent. I explained to him that if I had had a program like this when I was 18, things would have been much easier for me. Perhaps I would not have experienced so many painful hills that grew into mountains.

The work I did was exemplary; both Rob and his mother thought I was a dynamo. Rob's mother was the co-founder of the company: a tough businesswoman who was highly critical and skeptical of any consultant. I had to prove myself with this woman, and I did. She couldn't believe how quickly I could synthesize and develop systems that made so much sense. We got acquainted, and it would be a relationship that would lead to something very significant in the years to come.

Just months after I did the consulting work, Rob called me. I could not believe my ears; he wanted me to run a summer transition program as part of The Life Development Institute for 10 weeks in Phoenix. That meant I would develop curricula, deliver the classes, and do student advising as well as activities with this group. It was a big job: I was excited beyond belief and scared to death! My practice was small enough that I could leave for a while and it would not suffer; we could make arrangements for my family to come out for much of the summer. For the rest of the summer, Justin would visit his father and Tess would stay with her dad, except for a few weeks during the summer when the kids and Paul or the kids by themselves would come to stay with me. I was fortunate; a woman whose daughter I had helped years ago lived in the area, and when she learned of my summer plans, she offered her home while they were out of town for the summer. What could be more perfect—experience in my field and a beautiful home in a world class resort where I could stay? My family would love it when they arrived. It all seemed too easy.

I presented the idea to my husband, who had his concerns, which mostly centered on how much this would cost over how much I would earn, but somehow we were able to work through it. We had other issues much worse than a job for the summer. I think back to the last 10 years we were together, all the problems we had, all the tears of joy and anger, and my own inner anger. My inability to provide for him what I had in the past financially was troubling; I thought perhaps this was why he didn't like me, so I would show him I was still capable. Even more was at stake: I had to do this for our children, for me, and for individuals who have hidden disabilities. Though no one can really understand, it is those people out there, the ones I have helped, the ones who have helped me, who keep me moving forward.

After I completed all of my tasks, I packed and headed for Phoenix in my car, on my own! I felt like a pioneer. As I was driving, it occurred to me: I had never really had an adventure in my adult life. I had had my kids so young, worked very hard from the time I was 16, had to grow up fast, and now I was headed out on my own with the feeling of hope and intrigue. I kept imagining with excitement and fear what the summer would hold. I kept telling myself that I had the ability to make a difference in these kids' lives, that I would give them the motivation to move ahead, to believe in themselves, and to have tools to use. I hoped one day that they would remember me as I remembered those who helped me.

When I arrived, I was tired but I fought it. I had driven a 13-hour day and a 15-hour day; my energy level was soaring. I jumped right in, got settled, and the next day I picked up my first student, Janet. This young woman was scared and "standoffish," and I could tell she was very worried about how she would do during the summer. Her perseveration was high, but we had a little extra time to get acquainted; class was not to start until Monday and it was Saturday. So, with her mother's permission, I took her with me to see my sister. This was another extraordinary aspect of my summer work and my decision to come to Arizona; my sister had moved there, and lived only 2 hours away. I was looking forward to spending some time with her and to having her come stay with me—perhaps a stronger bond of friendship could emerge! All the way down, Janet shared with me stories of her experiences, her anger, her fear; she expressed how she felt stupid, how she knew she would fail in this program, how she hated her life. My heart went out to her; I understood what she was saying; I could feel the intensity of her pain. Slowly she began to trust me; she stopped shaking so much, and she began to smile and laugh.

By the time Monday had rolled around and the other kids had arrived, Janet was singing the praises of her new teacher and her hopes for the summer. That week was probably one of the best I can remember having in a very long time. I was teaching them how to establish a system for group success—and they were learning it! Some of what I found worked best with these young adults was what I think we often forget when teaching or working with kids. I entered this summer with a lighthearted nature, an open mind, and a willingness to get creative. Having the ability to implement techniques and alternatives was critical in this role, and I had the ability to implement on a dime. Our classes were practical; we worked on how others perceived us, how we perceived ourselves, what we knew about our strengths, our interests, our values, and our desires for life. We explored our weaknesses in relationship to work, family, social skills, independent living, friendships, and our own internal feelings on this issue. The key word here is *we*; I allowed them to know that I, too, have learning disabilities. I, too, have walked down a frustrating road. I was part of them and they were part of me. They were enjoying it; when personalities would conflict, we would work through it successfully. We set up our class as a team, just like in a company. We all established our mission, our charter; and we determined our roles, our goals, and our standard operating procedures! We were determined to have success; we were all in this together. The beauty of it was that it worked along with the nurturing behavior I had; the one thing these kids were drawn to naturally was what I needed all those years, someone who believed in them, someone who genuinely cared about them.

That summer I learned a lot about myself. I also learned a lot about the strength of my marriage. It was the year of our tenth anniversary; I thought it was perfect: Paul's parents could keep the kids, and all it would cost was a $200 airplane ticket to come out. We could have a wonderful celebration at the Boulders (the location of my friend's house). I asked Paul to come out; he refused, claiming it was a waste of money. After all it would be just 2 weeks before he would come out anyway, and it was just a date, what was the big deal? I became hysterical. He didn't really seem to care how I was going to deal with this. His claims weren't justified; we had the money, but he couldn't spend a weekend with his wife on our anniversary. I realized at that moment I really wasn't loved.

I spent the weekend getting drunk by myself except when my friends came to see me. Thank goodness for friends. Paul didn't even send me a gift for our anniversary—nothing. The worst part about it was that he continued to dismiss my feelings of rejection and told me I was being overemotional because I wanted him to be there on our anniversary. The ultimate rejection!

But the summer was not a total waste. I learned that I could make an impact on a group of young people. Thanks to my friend Rob, I learned that I was fun to be around, and I learned that I could still work with people and be respected for my knowledge.

For some of us, finding reality means having to live many years in a nightmare, experiencing one disappointment after another. I happen to be one of those people—maybe it was because it just worked out that way, but more than likely it was because I had hidden disabilities. These disabilities placed me at risk for having more problems, more complications, more uncertainties, and more negative outcomes than the average person has. But something else I did learn was that perhaps I have expectations about others and myself that can be unrealistic. I have learned that I have to create my own happiness and teach my children to do the same. I think about them—how their lives will be as adults. They are both so much like me yet each is beautiful and unique. I sometimes worry that they will experience great pain and difficulty fitting in because others will not see them as honest or believable. But I know that I must teach them to carry on despite their own internal fears. Despite the pain I have experienced—the fact that I have learned that some people cannot be trusted—I refuse to give up. My dream is that one day we will learn to care about others who are different, not for our own self-serving purposes, but for the continued belief that the human race is equal. Everyone deserves the same opportunities that some of us have been given, and everyone is entitled to be understood.

After the first summer program, things began to make sense to me. I began to see that the world was very different than what I thought it should be. Perhaps I am a late bloomer, but bloom I did. For whatever reason—be it my attitude, my reputation, my hard work, the realization that the man I worshipped didn't feel the same about me, or a combination of all those things—I began to climb professionally, and most importantly, emotionally.

My family did come out that first summer 2 weeks after the

anniversary I spent alone. Paul even came out one more time, not because he thought of it on his own, but because he was encouraged to by my best friend Jim, who told him he had better come out because I was not doing well and needed him. Jim understood what I was going through because of his own difficulties in being accepted and understood; he knew what I was thinking and that it was just a matter of time before my marriage crumbled unless Paul started showing that he loved me genuinely. It wasn't far from the truth; the pain was just too much. I began to reflect on all the negative aspects of our relationship, his forgetting about me and how much I adored him. I began to be bitter. I needed to be loved and cared for and given lots of attention. I was slipping in and out of a horrible depression, feeling isolated and alone. The only time I felt appreciated was when I was working, and most of the time that I felt the most valued, I was on the road.

Two years went by. I did yet another summer program, and upon my return home, things just weren't the same. My hope that Paul and I could find love and work things out did not seem possible. Too many past mistakes had been made by both of us; there was too much sadness in myself and too little willingness on his part to change the things that I believed needed to be changed the most. It was all of this that would eventually lead to our failed marriage. Within the next year, we would file for divorce, I would move to Arizona, and there my life would change in ways I could never begin to imagine.

INSIGHTS AND INTERVENTIONS
by Larry B. Silver, M.D.

As a young professional woman, Veronica began to succeed. She learned more about her disabilities. She learned how to learn and experience success. She felt confident enough to be her own advocate.

This understanding and success gave her the opportunity to get to know herself from a different perspective. The healing process could begin.

I remember a conversation I had with Veronica about this time. Later I sent her a note. I urged her to get into therapy. I told her that she had to get inside her head and meet her monsters face-to-face. She needed to understand each monster. Each reflected her life experiences and fears; she was each of them. I explained that she would never find inner peace, that she could never successfully run away from her nightmares, until she could go up to each monster, face it eye-to-eye, embrace it, and say that she understood, while comforting each. Inner peace meant that she could love each monster. She could understand each based on the life they lived. As long as she fought them, they would remain. Once she could accept them, love them, and embrace them, they would heal and change from monsters to friends.

Slowly, through life experiences and successes and through hard, often painful inner work, she entered her nightmare and confronted her monsters. Slowly, she began to grow toward making peace with herself. Slowly, her self-esteem and self-image changed. It was only through this process that she could have her "awakening."

8

THE AWAKENING

HAPPY IN MY PRIME

Everyone has the ability to
be kind; kindness is one
skill you can learn, and the
one that is the most
valuable in life.

As I complete this book at the age of almost 40, I have reached the conclusion that I am not an easy person to get to know. Most people find me delightful in the work I do. I believe this is because they know I genuinely care, but deep down inside, I know that it is friendships and relationships with significant people in my life that give me the most sadness. Partly, this is because of my general personality, but mostly it is because I just seem to care too much and most people don't believe that is possible.

Sometimes I wonder: If I didn't have learning disabilities, would I have bipolar disorder? If I didn't have learning disabilities, would I still be working in the corporate setting? If I didn't have learning disabilities, would I be happier? I can't say that I have a definitive answer for these questions, but what I do have is experience, and it seems to me that in my life and in the lives of those I have met with similar challenges, these disabilities play tremendous havoc on one's daily life.

To know me today, most people would say that it appears that I have overcome my disabilities. I just grin, and my response is dictated by whomever is making the statement. Others tell me I am an inspiration; still others simply do not believe me. In the years since I moved to Phoenix I have learned more about myself than I ever thought possible. Much credit is due to my husband Rob, my friend whom I married not long ago. He understands me. He knows how to help me when I want to give up, when to calm me when I feel I can take on the world, and when to let me be alone when I need time to think. He is patient with me when I get lost (almost four times a week) and I call to report that I can't remember, for example, where my cosmetologist is located, even though I have been there eight times before. When I stand in the checkout line and can't remember the difference between a credit and a debit (after all, aren't they both deductions?). When I have to fill out any kind of form, look something up in the telephone book, or ask how to spell "disability" even though I spell it every day several times a day.

He knows when we are in a social situation and I just need to be a listener that it's not because I don't care, it's because I don't understand and am not comfortable asking questions. He knows that I am most comfortable in my working environment because I know that language well. He knows how to make me laugh and not cry. Most important, I finally figured out what love is. It's acceptance and never having to have the last, cutting word, but instead, giving the first loving hug.

Having hidden disabilities is far more complex than people want to admit. I am sure most people who read this book are wondering if my learning disabilities were caused by childhood traumas or if I was born that way, or maybe, because I moved around a lot. And I would ask them, how many other people who have had similar types of experiences don't have learning disabilities? Does it really matter what caused them? They exist.

No matter who you are, nothing is more difficult than being rejected, but being rejected because you are perceived as "different" or "slow" is nothing short of a crime. It is hard to understand what it must be like to have hidden disabilities if you don't have them, just like it would be hard to really know what it must be like to have millions of dollars and not know whom you can trust. I would suggest that no matter what one's "difference" is, all human beings have the same type of emotional response to the unknown—fear.

My life is really no easier today; I just understand it more. I know that for me to be successful at what I do I have to recognize that I have these hidden disabilities; I have to know what tools and resources work best for me; I have to know my limitations and my strengths. Most of all, I have to know that tomorrow I will wake up and find the same, if not more challenges, as the day before. And somehow I have to find a way to keep fighting for me, for those with whom I work, and for those who love me.

I am different than people without hidden disabilities, and some days I like it that way. Most days I wonder what might have been had I not had all these problems. Would I have had the confidence to wait for a man who really understood me? Would I have had the skills to finish a Ph.D.? Would I have friends in my life who really want to be around me? I am still so very lonely; I must tell you too, that most of the people I work with report the same loneliness. Does the sadness, the pain stop? The answers to these questions depend on me and on my reaction to the world. I know I have struggles; it is me who has to find the strength to go on. It's too bad really, but that, my dear friends, is what life is all about. We are all different; we are all unique and beautiful in our own way. Perhaps if you just try to be kind to one person a day—a stranger or even someone you know—you will be a hero that day. You may even save a life—of course you'll never know. Everyone has the ability to be kind; kindness is one skill you can learn, and the one that is the most valuable in life.

I ask you all to try to feel what it is like to be trapped in a mind of confusion. Imagine for a day what it would be like to have your same level of intelligence but your academic skills reduced to that of a fourth grader. Imagine what it would be like to have your processing skills changed so that when you receive an oral message, you miss every third word. Think what it would be like to have your short-term memory skills altered so that when you try to make an impression on someone, you can't remember his or her name for the fifth time. Try to imagine what it would be like to work in a job that you hated because you couldn't articulate your abilities well enough for someone to believe you really had the skills. Try to imagine being married to someone who tells you you're stupid— and you believe him. Perhaps then you will understand that people with hidden disabilities have just as valid and real concerns and challenges as do people who have visible disabilities. The only difference is the way it affects him or her, but the impact is the same. The person experiences loss of esteem, loss of hope, and loss of dreams.

Today I am doing well; I am in my sixth year of having my own business working with people like myself. I still use accommodations, including computer hardware and software such as textHelp for writing and reading, Kurzweil 3000 (for reading extensive works), and a Palm Pilot for organizing, remembering, and simplifying. I recognize that I owe a great deal of thanks to the department of vocational rehabilitation (VR), my husband for editing my materials, an array of people I hire to help me, or those who just help me out of the desire to do so. I am reaching my personal definition of success. I have finished this book, though as I write these words, my insecurity still crops up; with tears in my eyes I feel that I have forgotten something critical. I am also laughing about the fact that I can't even read my own book very easily—not in the traditional manner anyway. I hope that by sharing all of this pain and all of this success, I do not confuse you. My only hope is that readers will either find someone who can help them or find the strength in themselves to look in the mirror and realize that there is a way they can achieve success or help others with hidden disabilities do the same. It takes self-determination, realistic goals, and hard work. Most important, for readers who have hidden disabilities, the best way to start on the road to success and to achieve it is to give themselves credit for being human.

I am reminded of a statement made by someone who I believed to be a person with great insight and tremendous motivation, Helen Keller. She once said, "Character cannot be developed in ease and quiet. Only through experiences of trial and suffering can the soul be strengthened, vision cleared, ambition inspired, and success achieved." I know that for people with hidden disabilities, this statement will touch their hearts and show them that no matter what, they can succeed even when they face the worst of circumstances.

What I hope is that we all can learn to hold our heads high and realize there is a reason to always go on. I know the doubt is always going to be with me, as it will for most of us to some degree. Every day I wake up and still struggle to read, to write, to listen, and to remember. I realize it is a part of me, but *only* a part of me. There are days when it would be easier to give up, but I think of those who have inspired me, those who have believed in me, and I tell myself there is so much more that I have to offer. I owe it to myself and those who love me to give it my best.

The monster still lurks in the shadows, but now I know what to do about it. I just reach out my hand, gesture for it to come over, lean over, and say the words, "Veronica, I love you."

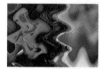

INSIGHTS AND INTERVENTIONS
by Larry B. Silver, M.D.

Gradually, Veronica began to understand herself and to like herself. Her inner strength made her less vulnerable to her outside world. Yes, she would experience frustrations and failures. Yes, she would experience criticism. We all do. But, she could reflect and say to herself, "I am a good person. I'm a capable person. I am smart. Yes, maybe I did something that could have been done better. But I am learning and I will improve." Each negative experience no longer threw her into depression. Equally important, with her growth she no longer needed relationships that reinforced her negative beliefs. She moved away from such relationships and realized that she deserved better.

Rob came into her life because she was ready for a person such as him. He accepted her as she was and supported her growth. He stayed close and shared her pain and stood tall praising her growth. Earlier in her life she would not have believed or accepted what he said and did. She would have thought, "If only he knew the real me..." But now, "the real me" was the real Veronica. She was open to share a positive relationship with someone who respected her and cared about her.

With this growth she could experience for the first time the true meaning of intimacy, which is made up of two parts. First is the ability to be close to someone. She always had this ability, though "close" often meant inviting verbal or emotional abuse. The second part of intimacy is the ability to be close to someone with whom you can enjoy mutual acceptance. You can disclose all and hear the other disclose all. Your love allows you to accept the other with all of his or her strengths and faults and you know the other accepts you with all of your strengths and faults. True intimacy with someone is not easy to obtain. It is the ultimate of life's beauties. Her book ends with a hint of her growing intimacy with Rob.

Veronica ends by telling us how she reached a point in her life when she could accept and love herself. She reached out to her monsters, held them, and told them that she loved them. With this inner communication, her nightmares ceased. There were no more monsters. At last she made peace with her painful past. Now, there could be a future.

Veronica and family: (from bottom left) Ciera, Tess, Devin; (from top left) Veronica, Erika, Justin, and husband Rob

9

TIPS AND TOOLS
THROUGH THE LIFE SPAN

WHAT TO LOOK FOR
AND HOW TO HELP

Many write off problems
to the concept that
"everyone develops
at a different pace."
I guess, to me, it's
wise to be cautious.
But when a child exhibits
too many signs, it may
indicate something much
more significant.

T his chapter is based on personal, reflective observations. It should be noted that these are not clinical observations: These signs are not always indicative of learning disabilities (LD), attention-deficit/hyperactivity disorder (ADHD), or sensory integration disorder. If, however, you see these signs it could be a warning to seek out professional assistance and a full psycho-educational, age-appropriate diagnostic workup by a licensed professional. Also, it is important that the professional you choose has training and certification in diagnosing and treating these disabilities. Always interview the professional; be aware of his or her training and background, and have a comfort level with the individual.

AGE-RELATED TIPS AND TOOLS

As you read through these tips and tools, remember that they are suggestions, not remedies. Seek professional assistance; this is your best option.

The Early Childhood Years

Today, more than in the past, we have a greater understanding of young children's problems and challenges. We can recognize certain warning signs that could help us to help our children. It is very important to recognize and not ignore these behaviors in early childhood. Be alert; keep a journal of the child's behaviors and look for patterns and trends. Here are some signs that parents, child care workers, family members, babysitters, and health care providers may want to watch for and note in a journal. These signs are only offered as observations, and remember, these are not sure signs that anything is wrong.

TIPS: WHAT TO LOOK FOR

You may want to seek professional guidance if you observe that your child

- Seems easily disturbed, not because of fatigue, hunger, or illness, or from having a basic human need unattended, but rather the child exhibits an obvious behavior that seems to follow him or her in every environment
- Seems mesmerized by lights, wanting to switch them on and off over and over to an almost obsessive degree
- Responds negatively to loud noises, not just sudden noises, but those that most children seem to enjoy
- Fights having tags on certain items of clothing or fabrics, complaining or indicating all the time that he or she is wearing them that they are irritating
- Frequently gives inappropriate responses to questions, such as answering "milk" when the appropriate response would be "juice"
- Seems to have excessive interest in an area in which he or she excels, but difficulty in areas that should be simple to master
- Has difficulty adjusting to change, even a change in the place in which to sit for dinner
- Withdraws or overreacts when there is a lot of activity going on, such as a holiday, a trip to the mall, or a circus
- Shows frustration on a regular basis when issues of language are involved
- Is a perfectionist; keeps his or her room perfect, doesn't want to get dirty
- Has difficulty with walking, riding a tricycle, bouncing a ball, throwing a ball, jumping, running, holding utensils, drawing, making shapes, doing puzzles, learning a routine (age-appropriate)

TOOLS: WHAT MAY HELP

1. Seek professional guidance from someone who is trained in any of these professions: pediatric neurologist, pediatric psychiatrist, pediatric psychologist. A pediatrician can help with

referrals to these professionals. Make sure you ask whether the person has specialized training in LD, ADHD, and sensory integration disorder.

2. Review the many books and Internet resources on LD, ADHD, and sensory integration disorder.

3. Seek out professional associations (see Resources) for recommendations of professionals in your area who specialize in these disabilities, local support groups, literature, seminars, schools, services, and legal counsel recommendations.

The Early Elementary Years

I think it would be easy to make a mistake and miss something in a child who has learned at a young age to pretend to be happy, a child who just seems a little different. Many write off problems to the concept that "everyone develops at a different pace." I guess, to me, it's wise to be cautious. But when a child exhibits too many signs, it may indicate something much more significant. I will again offer the perspective of someone who lives this life and works with people who live this life to provide my insights on what you may want to look for in your child. If you feel the least bit suspicious, go for an evaluation from a trained professional who specializes in the age group your child falls into. Also, there are many wonderful books, videos, and Internet sources out there on how to recognize the signs from the professionals' view.

TIPS: WHAT TO LOOK FOR

You may want to seek professional guidance if your child

- Is always on the go, is bored easily even when it is a game or activity that is enjoyable
- Is oversensitive to noise, light, certain activities, or events that have a lot of commotion
- Exhibits unusual acting-out behaviors or drastic changes in behavior

- Was once happy; is now quiet and withdrawn
- Has difficulty grasping age-appropriate academic levels; mixes letters, numbers, and symbols; knows something one day, not the next
- Is reported to daydream by teachers, parents, and family members
- Fears going to school; tries to find ways of not going to school
- Is compliant, overly anxious to please teachers or those who are in a position to determine ability
- Demonstrates physical pain when writing; hand or wrist hurts. Shakes off and massages wrist and/or hand when writing, takes frequent breaks. Presses very hard to write; has sloppy writing
- Whines and complains about homework or school on a frequent basis. Makes statements such as, "I can't do it," "I *am* trying," "I don't want to do it"
- Feels excessive anxiety over upcoming or unplanned events or school projects
- While trying to concentrate on something, is easily annoyed by little things others would not notice
- Expresses observations about being different from others; makes constant comparisons to friends, siblings, and other people who seem to do well
- Has difficulty remembering events, facts, dates, people's names, and places
- Is a great storyteller, or is frequently accused of lying or stretching the truth
- Tries hard, but still does not "get it"
- Shows extreme strengths in some areas despite extreme weaknesses in other areas; is a paradox
- Feels awkward, unloved, or unappreciated but has difficulty expressing these feelings (Kids with LD may not contribute after several failures in participating in group dynamics, even in their own families, which may cause them to withdraw from everything.)

- Exhibits dazed or almost trance-like behavior (It should be noted that this could also be a sign of a seizure disorder and it would be worth having the child evaluated by a neuropediatric psychiatrist.)
- Shows talent in an area but is unwilling or unmotivated to take risks with that talent
- Exhibits self-destructive behaviors in these or other areas: eating, drugs, alcohol, friends; shows a preference for solitude; talks about death or taking unnecessary risks

Others involved in this child's life, such as teachers, tutors, and parents, might also report

- Frustration regarding the child, for example, while trying to teach academics
- That this child is annoying, acts like a pest, a troublemaker, or is just too active. Gets on people's nerves. You might hear someone say things such as, "This child makes me angry," ". . . nervous," ". . . uneasy," or ". . . frustrated." You might hear this frequently, not just in school but in many environments.

TOOLS: WHAT MAY HELP

1. Remember that children with hidden disabilities often are overstimulated by too many choices. Narrow down options for decisions such as what to wear, where to go, what to see, or when to go to bed. The only caution is to offer only two options, otherwise overload can occur, and you might exacerbate the child's indecision.
2. Keep the child's environment free of too many knick-knacks, wall hangings, intense colors, or lights. Make the environment as clear of "stuff" as possible. Keep things neat and organized; it will help reduce the response to overstimulation.
3. Teach the child to keep a calendar; try a big dry-erase board or calendar. It is helpful for many of these kids. Record events,

activities, chores, homework, test dates, anything so the child can see it each morning and each evening to help him or her reduce anxiety and plan better.

4. Do not overwhelm the child with too many after-school activities. These children need down time—time to relax, read, watch television, play outside, do what calms them. Create a balance; if there is too much activity, they will have difficulty managing their behaviors independently.

5. If a child says he or she feels stupid, don't dismiss such feelings. Let the child talk about it, and validate these feelings. Then, discuss the child's real strength by giving examples he or she can relate to and believe.

6. Let the child know you believe in him or her; help the child to understand him- or herself. Talk with the child. Be a charismatic, empathetic person in his or her life.

7. Look for talents and help the child to develop those talents. Sometimes we don't expect a hobby to be an area of talent, but look at the skills necessary for having this hobby; they may provide clues to these children's hidden strengths.

8. If a child seems frustrated with doing homework, let him or her take a short break, with the understanding that the child needs to return to the homework at the end of that break.

9. Try not to lose patience when you are working to help a child understand something. If you believe that you cannot control your temper, look to have someone else—perhaps a tutor or another family member—assist him or her.

10. Showcase that child as much if not more than other siblings. Build the child's self-esteem.

11. Don't be afraid to begin discussing drugs, alcohol, and sexuality issues early on. These children will face the same issues as any young person, but be aware that the temptations may be greater due to these children's lowered self-esteem, or they may be vulnerable to self-medicating with drugs, alcohol, and other dangerous behaviors.

Remember that these are just suggestions of things to watch for. Always be certain to check with a licensed diagnostician to determine if there is a problem. Too often we jump to conclusions before we have all the facts; this list is simply to alert you to look into the possibilities so that professionals such as myself can assist you as needed.

The Teen Years

As a person who has walked in these shoes as a teen I can offer you the following tips. Let these be alerts, not necessarily an indication that someone has LD, ADHD, or another hidden disability but warning signs to seek help or understanding from a trained professional. If you believe a teenager might have a problem, seek someone who works with adolescents and can determine if it might be psychological, physiological, or typical teenage behavior.

TIPS: WHAT TO LOOK FOR

You may want to seek professional guidance if your teenager

- Begins to withdraw from you, the family, and/or things he or she used to enjoy
- Seems down, depressed, unmotivated, or doesn't seem to have the same energy as he or she used to
- Exhibits behavioral changes; for example, he or she used to love to sit and watch television and now only wants to sleep, or he or she used to be neat but now is very sloppy
- Appears to have an extreme need for control in his or her life
- Seems to be choosing unhealthy relationships—these can be friendships or dating relationships
- Is being sneaky, sly, or manipulative
- Avoids doing any homework; books stay in the backpack all night or the teen might tell you every day that there is no homework

- Demonstrates unwillingness to read out loud to you or do other academic types of activities, such as reading instructions to play a game
- Experiences excessive changes in diet and exercise
- Shows indications that he or she may be using drugs or alcohol
- Starts skipping school or certain classes, fakes illness at times
- Expresses no hope in his or her future or doesn't know what he or she is good at; sees no ability in him- or herself or feels like a failure
- Has difficulty sitting still, keeping focused, paying attention to everything
- Daydreams a lot
- Demonstrates extreme irritability, becomes annoyed easily, is hypercritical of self and others

TOOLS: WHAT MAY HELP

1. Set consistent expectations and consequences for your teen. The best situation is not to surprise him or her with any sudden changes, good or bad.
2. Make an appointment for your teenager to meet with a transition specialist, a personal coach, or a career counselor. He or she needs to start identifying strengths and weaknesses in terms of career choices. Your teenager also needs to start looking at educational and training programs for career preparation and training, as well as specialized services to help him or her enhance skills.
3. Help the teenager to see options without overwhelming him or her with the details. Let the teenager begin to explore the pros and cons of certain behaviors.
4. Encourage independence but teach responsibility for appropriate behavior and the consequences he or she may face from outside sources.

5. Don't be afraid to say "no." He or she is just like any other teen and has the same temptations and interest in trying new things, including things that could be harmful. Set guidelines and teach the teenager about drugs, sex, peer pressure, and other sensitive issues.

6. Have regular talks with him or her about school, friends, and activities.

7. Give the teenager responsibilities, such as preparing a meal, cleaning up, or doing laundry.

8. Give the teenager freedom to be independent, but let him or her know your expectations.

9. Encourage the teenager to take calculated risks, and let him or her know that calculated risks are healthy for learning.

10. Let the teenager explore his or her fears and frustrations, but always keep an open-door attitude if your child needs you.

11. Understand that he or she may be embarrassed about accommodations now, but that they are nothing more than the means of providing equal opportunities for success. Ask your child for suggestions on what else may help.

Young Adult and Adult Years

I feel as though it is important to stress again that these are just my ideas on what to look for—some warning signs. It is important to remember that only an expert can diagnose a disability such as LD or ADHD, as well as any other psychological or physiological problems, but if we have ideas on what to look for, then perhaps it will serve a helpful purpose.

TIPS: WHAT TO LOOK FOR

A person may have hidden disabilities if he or she

- Perseverates or focuses on a subject or issue that has long since passed. This is usually something that no one else cares about except the person in question, who can't forget about it.

- Feels inadequate, that he or she can't do anything right
- Experiences difficulty in jobs or in relationships, which seems to form a pattern
- Is unorganized or overorganized to a degree that it is affecting his or her life and the ability to accomplish other things
- Is uncertain of abilities or unrealistic about abilities
- Experiences multiple failures in school, jobs, and relationships
- Abuses alcohol or drugs
- Exhibits physically, emotionally, or financially risky behaviors
- Has few friends or support systems; prefers to be alone or tells you that is so
- Has no goals established for the future; is dependent on someone or something in an unrealistic or unhealthy way
- Has low self-esteem; shows depressive tendencies
- Has extreme difficulty staying on task
- Does not or will not read even for enjoyment
- Makes an excuse about why he or she doesn't want to go to college or a trade school
- Tries to find other ways to succeed that are unhealthy and unrealistic
- Seeks out others to fill out forms, handle checking account, help with paperwork
- Doesn't appear to be motivated to create change in his or her life
- Describes self as being dumb, unable, or lazy

TOOLS: WHAT MAY HELP

If someone you know and care about fits these characteristic signs, here are some ways you can help:

1. Encourage the individual to seek the advice of a professional specializing in adult testing for LD and ADHD.
2. Seek out the services offered by the local vocational rehabilitation (VR) office, a federal program for adults with disabilities.
3. Put the person in touch with literacy groups.

4. Seek out organizations and associations listed under adult services.

5. Support the individual when he or she is feeling down. Let the person know that it is very possible to learn to manage these disabilities. Let him or her know that he or she has obviously been compensating very well without help for years; imagine how, with the help of others, the person can do even more.

6. Teach skills in the area of executive functioning, which includes time management, organization, and appropriate interpersonal behaviors.

7. Suggest that the person receive counseling support to help understand how to work through the pain.

8. Give the individual clear examples of famous and "regular" people with hidden disabilities who are successful.

9. Find local adult support groups.

10. Let the individual know you understand and will always lend an ear.

The College or University Years

Here are some ideas on what to look for in a college or university that worked for me.

1. Choose a school in which the classes are relatively small. You need to have the instructor's attention, and the smaller the class, the more likely you are to get it.

2. Choose a school in which there are more full-time faculty and fewer adjunct professors. You need to have access to these people on a more frequent basis, if possible. Adjunct professors are less likely to have office hours for students.

3. Choose a school that has a disability services department with staff who have experience in helping people with LD and ADHD.

4. Have a list of questions to ask of the disability services employees related to your specific disability and the types of accommodations that have worked for you.

5. Check on the availability of these supports and accommo-dations and ask whether others have used similar tools. Ask what type of success those students had with them.

6. Through disability services, find out what the process is for notifying professors that you have a disability and seek advice on what other information these professors might need.

7. Find out if the disability services department encourages individuals to advocate for themselves along with the support the department provides, and how receptive others are to this self-advocacy.

8. Find out how soon professors' syllabi are printed and when you could get access to them, as well as the required reading and assignments for the classes.

9. Find out what the requirements are for the degree you are seeking and determine, if needed, alternate classes that may be taken. These alternate classes would need to be determined on an individual and degree program basis.

10. Find out what services students use most frequently while in college, how many students who use the services actually graduate from this college, and where they go after graduating.

11. Determine whether you can work with the people in the disability services department. Are you comfortable with them? Will they be able to advocate for you if there is a crisis? Do they have a commitment to your success?

12. Locate a mentor or coach in the area to assist you with personal, educational, and career issues using specific goal-setting and application strategies.

TOOLS FOR POSTSECONDARY SUCCESS

Once you have chosen the right college or university, here are some tips on getting through the postsecondary years:

1. Look at the class schedule. Determine what classes you have to take. This was extremely important to do; many times I

would look at the previous semester's schedule to try and predict what types of classes would be offered the next semester. I always had a mapped sheet with the required classes so I knew what I needed for the course of study I was taking.

2. Balance the classes; put in at least one class that would not require any papers or heavy study requirements, yet make sure you are still able to carry 12 hours. For example, a workable schedule might be one history class, one psychology class, one music class, and perhaps a science class. I was strong in music and psychology, so the other two would be my most challenging. A balance was created.

3. Discuss classes and instructors with the disability services department and determine what best suits your learning style. Of course I had to know what my best learning style was, and I knew that I succeeded better with instructors who did not focus strictly on lectures. It was much easier for me to be in a class with many class discussions and projects and tests written in essay form. I also needed an instructor who really loved teaching, enjoyed a challenge, and had an open mind.

4. Register for the classes early. Always use the preregistration option; most colleges and universities have this for students with disabilities. This way one gets first pick of the classes being offered. Furthermore, the potential humiliating and embarrassing situations that arise from being in line are eliminated.

5. Set up appointments with the instructors as much in advance as possible. There wasn't a semester when I did not have at least 2 to 3 weeks prior to class to meet with the instructors. This gave me the advantage: They had met me, we had worked out the accommodation issues, and I knew what would be expected of me.

6. Explain the purpose of the meeting by telling the instructors why you want to meet them and how you can be successful in

their class. This is critical. This may take some courage if you are anxious about starting a conversation and unsure of how the person will respond to your requests. I always used the theory that these instructors have needs just like I have needs.

7. Get the syllabus, or at least the required reading, textbook name, and major projects in advance.

8. Get all required reading on tape. Begin researching projects and narrow down resources. Set up tutors and notetakers if needed.

9. Get a head start on reading and notetaking from text.

10. Always go to every class. Sit in the front row.

11. Make arrangements with disability services and instructors to take tests outside of class, if needed.

12. Follow up at all times. Keep a very organized calendar and materials.

13. Follow due dates and set study time lines.

CHOOSING A CAREER

I have found that it is important to spend time looking at one's strengths and weakness when considering a career. In the work I do, several tools are useful to help people determine a realistic and desired career choice. This is a sample of the steps one should consider once an interest/aptitude/ability/values assessment has been conducted.

Determine Strengths and Weaknesses

It is helpful to make out list of strengths and weaknesses such as the one below:

Strengths	Weaknesses
Communicates well (orally, in writing)	Memory recall of terms
	Sequencing
Organized	Poor spelling
Analytical	Poor punctuation and grammar
Logical	skills

Decisive	Poor reading/comprehension
Energetic	Hyperactive
Independent	Poor math skills
Creative	Insecure (known only to self)
	Poor handwriting

Determine Requirements

Then we look at what a specific job requires (this example is for a development trainer):

Required skills
Organizational skills
Written skills (content)
Research skills
Negotiation skills
Group processing
 skills
Facilitation skills
Presentation skills
Oral communication
 skills
Computer skills

Required education/training
Minimum bachelor's degree
2+ years related experience
Education and or experience in:
 adult learning theories
 career development
 team development
 computers
 human behavior
 employment law
 presenting/teaching/training

Match Strengths to Requirements

Once strengths are listed, then match strengths to the requirements listed:

Strengths	**Requirements**
Organized	Organizational skills
Communicates well (orally)	Presentation skills
Analytical/logical	Research/negotiation/group processing/facilitation skills
Decisive	Group processing/research negotiation/facilitation
Energetic	Presentation/group skills
Communicates well (written)	Research/writing
Independent	Negotiation/facilitation/ decision making
Creative	Presentation/decision making/ group skills

Match Background with Requirements

Next, it is important to determine whether you have the right educational background for a job. Again, making a list can be helpful:

Possess	Required
B.A. in Psychology	B.A. + adult learning & human behavior
4 years of training	2+ years related experience in presenting and teaching
	Employment law
	Career development
	Team development

Obviously, there are some education and training areas that an individual still might need but the links have been established. Therefore, one would need to consider steps to get to this point. These are some things I would need to do to get into this type of position:

1. Continue my education. Get a master's degree in human resources with a focus on training and development. Be sure to take classes that also focus on career development, team building, organizational development, and employment law.
2. Get a position with a company that would hire me as a recruiter with the ability to help the training and development department on a limited basis.
3. Get on-the-job training using computers for enhanced capabilities.
4. Become more familiar with employment laws through education, on-the-job training, and self-study.
5. Work hard at all times, be open, recognize strengths, and learn to find alternatives or accommodations for weaknesses. Those weaknesses should be listed with appropriate accommodations. Here is an example of a list of concerns and modifications:

Concerns	Accommodation/Modification
Memory recall of terms	Use notes/or overheads for areas that would pose a problem.
	Disclose that this is a problem and be prepared to give possible solutions for solving any complications that could occur.
	Define the terms, explain them without using the exact terms, use the concept.
	Keep a sheet of terms you are likely to forget.
Unorganized	Use organizational tools such as: calendars/handheld computers, wall organizers, color-coded files
	Develop system for self
	Use stacking bins
	Plan days in advance/work overtime
	Keep all notes/file everything
Poor spelling	Always have someone proof work
	Disclose the problem to appropriate people
	Use a spell check on computer
	Carry a handheld computer with spell check
Punctuation	Use word processing system tools
	Have someone proof all work
	Always take your time
Reading comprehension	Get materials in advance
	Disclose problem to appropriate people
	Get materials on tape if possible
	Leave extended time to read
	Have someone explain when there is not time to read it/take notes
Hyperactivity	Look into medication to help
	Explain need for short breaks to key people privately
	Explain need to stand and work or move while working
	Consider the environment to anticipate problems
Poor math skills	Have a calculator at all times
	Have a methods sheet
	Ask for assistance
Poor handwriting	Don't worry about it so much; many people have this problem
	Use the computer (a laptop if possible)
	Have someone else do the writing

| Hidden insecurity | Find someone who could be a positive mentor/coach to help with confusion
Continue in therapy |
| Impulsiveness and inattention | Medication for ADHD may be an option
Stay away from areas that are over-stimulating. Try to pick meeting areas that are less distracting. Try to set up work that is more redundant during times when you are more naturally alert. |

DISCLOSING HIDDEN DISABILITIES

Talking about a hidden disability is not easy; after all, to some people, that indicates weakness and no one wants to discuss that. There is a way, however, to reduce the odds. First, present all of your abilities, how you would perform the essential functions of the job, then present ideas on how to enhance the job. Finally, mention elements of the job in which you would use tools that made you so successful in your education (or training) and explain the purpose in using those tools. A healthy way to disclose is to tell them in these steps:

TOOLS FOR DISCLOSURE

1. Discuss what you *can* do, how you are qualified to do the job.
2. Discuss how you will go about doing the job.
3. Describe how you would enhance the job.
4. Mention tools you have used that could be integrated into the requirements of the job.
5. Discuss why you would use those tools, explaining the specific disability as it relates to the job, how such tools made you so much more successful in what you did previously, and how you would use them in your job.

Of course, you only need to disclose what is necessary. For example, if you would not be doing any math that would be affected by your specific disability or would need an accommodation, there is no need to mention it. You only disclose when you know you will need an accommodation to perform the essential functions of the job for which you are qualified to perform.

Know your rights under the law. Study the Americans with Disabilities Act (ADA) of 1990 (PL 101-336) and Section 504 of the Rehabilitation Act of 1973 (PL 93-112). The ADA and Section 504 are the two laws that protect adults with disabilities. Seek assistance from federal programs, consultants, disability service providers, the Internet, and the library for more information on these laws. Keep in mind, however, that as people with disabilities, we have rights but we also have responsibilities. We still have to meet the requirements of the job, perform the essential functions with or without accommodations, and follow the company policies. We deserve the same rights as any worker but we must also realize that we must perform like any worker as well; we simply utilize reasonable accommodations. And remember, the term *reasonable* means just that; the employer and the employee need to agree about the most reasonable accommodation that does not affect other workers' ability to do their job or have an impact on a company in a substantial way. Again, review the information on the ADA as it pertains to people with LD and ADHD.

It is very important to determine if and when disclosure of disability is needed. My personal rule of thumb is that disclosure is needed when you know your disability is going to get you into performance difficulties and you cannot self-manage, and any performance difficulties would be a direct result of a documented disability that is substantial in nature. This is when a reasonable accommodation should be considered by you and the employer to help you be successful in your position. Remember, when you do have to disclose, do it in writing as well as verbally, and make recommendations as to what would help you to be successful. Finally, remember that it must not pose an undue hardship on the company.

TOOLS FOR EMPLOYERS

Below are some tips on how to be a good manager or supervisor of a person with LD and/or ADHD. These are just a few suggestions:

1. When an employee or potential employee discloses that they have LD, don't act surprised. Be understanding. If you don't understand it, ask if the person can explain it to you. Ask how you can help him or her be a successful employee, and show the person where help and accommodations can be found.
2. Be kind. Build a relationship of trust and honesty.
3. Be supportive and encouraging, redirect in private, and always recognize a job well done.
4. Be clear about your expectations.
5. Put any materials in writing and explain them to your employee.
6. Follow up on any comments or promises you have made to that person.
7. Always look for ways this person could grow and be challenged; he or she doesn't want a situation in which there is no hope for growth in the future.
8. Encourage the person to continue to develop his or her job skills. Give regular, effective feedback and help him or her find ways to do tasks that are useful and applicable.
9. If there is a need for others to know about this, ask the person how he or she would like it to be handled.
10. Be fair and equitable in the way you treat all of your employees. Base promotions and raises on measurable performance.
11. Always be open to questions or concerns. Though you may find them tiresome at times, try to remember those questions and concerns come from someone who wants to succeed.

10

UNDERSTANDING HIDDEN DISABILITIES

A ROAD MAP

Larry B. Silver, M.D.

It is not unusual for
children, adolescents, or
adults to have
one or more of
these disorders.
The more of these
hidden disorders
one has, the more likely
that others exist
or will manifest
themselves in time.

Throughout this book, Veronica refers to having language, learning, and motor disabilities as well as attention-deficit/hyperactivity disorder (ADHD). As an adult, she also was diagnosed with bipolar disorder. To fully understand her book, it is necessary to understand these disorders. They are related—but very different. They are invisible disabilities in that the person looks perfectly typical; thus, they are often missed. Often the attendant characteristics of these disorders are seen as voluntary and controllable: If the person only tried harder, he or she wouldn't have difficulties. These disabilities are not voluntary, however. They are real; they are neurologically based; and they cannot be corrected by trying harder. I start with a brief outline for understanding the pattern of disabilities she experiences. Then, I expand on each of the disabilities she struggles with.

UNDERSTANDING NEUROLOGICALLY BASED DISABILITIES

A learning disability is a neurological disorder. That is, it is the result of a nervous system that has been "wired" a little differently. The brain is clearly not damaged, defective, or retarded. But, in certain areas it processes information in a different way than it is supposed to. There are other problems relating to brain function that might exist along with learning disabilities. The term used for problems that might coexist with another problem is *comorbid.*

It is important to know of these related problems. Many children, adolescents, and adults with learning disabilities have comorbid problems. They, too, must be found and addressed. In this book, Veronica describes having many of the problems to be discussed. I find it helpful to have an overview or road map for making sense of these problems. There may be a reason that these problems are seen in the same person. I occasionally have parents say to me that no one seems to know what is wrong with their child. Every professional they see has a different diagnosis.

Often, the child *does* have several areas of difficulty, and each professional is focused on one of them.

Let me share my road map. For many children, something affects the brain early in development, often during the first part of their mother's pregnancy. When this happens, it is unlikely that only one area of the brain is involved. Several areas might be affected. To make it easier to study these individuals, professionals separate out each possible problem area and label it. So, depending on which areas of the brain are involved, the person will have different disorders.

For at least 50% of individuals, this developmental impact is the result of his or her genetic code. The problems run in these people's families because the genetic code tells these individuals' brains to wire themselves differently. We do not have a full explanation for the other 50%. I discuss some of these possibilities later in this chapter.

Before I become specific, let me explain another theme needed to understand hidden disabilities. The brain is immature at birth. It constantly grows by having new wires activated and fired. We call these *maturational spurts.* This growth takes place throughout childhood, adolescence, and early adulthood. Each maturational spurt is like going to a computer store and buying a software package. You install it in your computer and suddenly the computer can do things it could not do before. So it is, too, with each firing of new wires in the brain; the brain can do things it could not do before. As each new area is activated, there are two possibilities. It may be that the wires in this area were not affected initially and are wired "normally." Thus, when this area of the brain begins to work, the individual suddenly can do things that were difficult before. It is also possible that when this area of the brain begins to work, it will be apparent that this area is also wired differently, but we had no way of knowing until the area began to work. For these individuals, new problems arise.

This is the reason that some children struggle and struggle, then suddenly master things that were difficult before. For the professional working with a child at that time, this can be quite rewarding: He or she gets the credit for it. You have heard the stories: Mary struggled with reading for several years. Finally, she got Mrs. Jones as a teacher, and within a month she was reading. This is also the reason why some children improve in one area, only to find another area of difficulty.

The cortex or thinking part of the brain has many functions. For our discussion, I will say that there are four basic functions: 1) language skills, 2) muscle (i.e., motor) skills, 3) thinking (i.e., cognitive) skills, and 4) organization (i.e., executive function) skills. Any or all of these areas might be wired differently.

If the area of the brain that is wired differently relates to language functions, the person will have a problem called a *language disability.* The first clue often is a delay in language development. The child is not speaking by age 2, and by age 2½ or 3, the child is using only a few words. In some children their language development might not have improved by age 4. If speech and language therapists work with such a child, then it might be possible to speed up his or her language development. In this case parents breathe a sigh of relief. By the time the child is age 4 or 5, however, another problem might arise. This child may have difficulty proc-essing and understanding what is being said (called a *receptive language disability*); or he or she might have difficulty organizing thoughts, finding the right words, or speaking in a fluid and clear way (called an *expressive language disability*). More help is needed.

As this child enters the early elementary grades, yet another problem might become apparent. The first task in reading is language-based. The child must recognize units of sound (called *phonemes*) and connect this sound to the correct unit of symbols (called *graphemes*). There are approximately 44 phonemes in the English lan-guage. Each letter has a sound, vowels have two sounds (a short and a long sound), and certain combinations (e.g., *sh, th, ch*) have their own sounds. The graphemes in the English

216

language are represented by 36 symbols used alone or together (26 for A–Z and 10 for 0–9). To learn to read, a child must learn to break this code by learning what sounds go with what symbols and sounding out words. Many children with delays in language development and later with receptive and/or expressive language problems have difficulty with learning to read in the first grade. Spelling is the reverse process. One must start with the language in one's brain and connect it with the right symbols by writing on the page. Thus, many children with reading problems also have problems with spelling.

It is easy to see, then, that some children have a delay in language, receive help, improve, and never have another problem. Others might improve but later receptive and expressive language problems show up. With help, *these* problems may improve and the child might have no further problems. Other children, however, progress from language problems to reading problems. It just depends on whether the next area of brain activation is also wired differently.

If the area of an individual's brain that is wired differently relates to the use of muscles, he or she will have what is called a *motor disability*. For some, the primary problem relates to the ability to coordinate and use teams of large muscles (called *gross motor skills*), and they will have difficulty running, jumping, or climbing. Others might have difficulty coordinating and using teams of small muscles (called *fine motor skills*). They have difficulty with learning to button, zip, tie, color within the line, use scissors, use eating utensils, and later, with using a pencil or pen to form letters and to write. Still others might have a broader pattern of motor problems called *sensory integration dysfunction.* Now, in addition to gross and fine motor planning functions, they might have difficulty making sense out of information coming from nerve endings in the skin. They might be very sensitive to touch or misread temperature or pain. They also might have difficulty processing information from their inner ear (i.e., the *vestibular* system), information that indicates where the body is in relation to gravity. They have difficulty with movement in space or position in space. Which of these many possible motor problems are present will depend on the area of the brain involved.

If the area of the brain that is wired differently relates to the processing of information for learning, we call it a *learning disability*. In some ways, this division of the cortex is artificial. If an individual has a learning disability, more than one area of the brain is involved.

The most recent addition to the cortex is the sophisticated area of the brain that acts like the chief executive officer in a company. This area carries out what is called *executive functions*. It orchestrates behaviors. This is the area that assesses a task or problem, decides how to tackle or solve the task, orchestrates the necessary activities or function, continually makes mid-course changes or corrections, and eventually reaches a successful conclusion. If this area of the brain is involved, we see people who have difficulty with organizational planning and carrying out tasks successfully.

This problem with wiring might extend beyond the cortex. There is an area of the brain that is often called the area of "vigilance." This is the area of the brain found in animals and primitive humans as well as in modern humans. It is the area that allows us to hunt. It gives us the ability to sit very still so that we do not scare away prey and the ability to track and prey and not be distracted by any background activity. It also gives us the ability to strike just at the right time. This is not only a human trait. Picture, for example, a frog sitting on a lily pond; not a muscle moves or the fly will go away. The eyes track the fly without losing sight. And, just at the right moment, the tongue comes out and catches the fly. Some children have problems with the wiring of this area of vigilance. As a result, they might be hyperactive, distractible, or impulsive. We call this disorder attention-deficit/hyperactivity disorder (ADHD).

This road map is somewhat sketchy. But, you can see why some children have a learning disability. Others might have a language disability or sensory integration dysfunction. Still others might have ADHD. For many, they might have one, two, three, or all four of these problems. These children do not have multiple disorders. They are manifesting multiple examples of the initial underlying problem that resulted in areas of the brain being wired differently.

With the dramatic new methods for studying the brain, other problem areas are starting to make sense. We have another area of the brain that might be called the *modulation* area. This is the area that maintains a balance or equilibrium, avoiding extremes. As we study this area, we find that there are many functions that need to be modulated. If any specific area is involved, we find a problem with modulation of specific function. Because the problem has been there since birth, the specific modulating problem also has been there since birth. Some people have problems *modulating anxiety.* They have a history since early life of being high strung or anxious. Over the years, the focus of the anxiety may change but the central theme is a high anxiety level. They might be afraid to go to sleep alone at night. Later, it might be a fear of being in part of the house alone or a fear of bees or a fear of something else. As these children move into adolescence or adulthood, they might develop a full *anxiety disorder.* Some may have so much difficulty regulating anxiety that the level gets too high and triggers off a physical response (i.e., fight or flight) called a *panic disorder.* They may break out into a sweat, their hearts may pound, and they may feel weak.

Another regulating problem relates to the ability to modulate anger. These children have been more irritable and angry since early childhood. They have always had tantrums. As they get older they show a specific form of difficulty regulating anger called an *intermittent explosive disorder.* In adolescence, a very few may show difficulty modulating not only the down side (depression) but also the up side (e.g., excitement, manic behavior). For these individuals their condition might evolve into a bipolar disorder (formerly called *manic-depressive disorder*).

Another pattern of behavior that seems to relate to these modulating disorders relates to the ability to regulate thoughts and behaviors. Some individuals have difficulty controlling their thoughts and experience the need to constantly repeat a thought or thought pattern to themselves (called *obsessive behavior*). Others might have difficulty regulating behaviors. They feel they must do certain things or they will get too anxious. They might believe that "it is silly" but they cannot stop. They might need to touch things a certain way or a number of times. They might need to check and recheck things (e.g., if the front door is locked or the stove is off). They might need to do certain patterns or rituals. This disorder is called *obsessive-compulsive disorder.*

One last area of difficulty with modulation may or may not turn out to be part of this pattern. This problem is a comorbid condition and relates to difficulty regulating certain motor functions. In individuals who experience such difficulty in modulation, clusters of muscles contract, causing what are called *motor tics.* Others may experience the need to say certain sounds or words, which is called an *oral tic.* These individuals have a tic disorder or a specific form of this problem, called *Tourette syndrome.*

Our brain, then, is a beautifully functioning, fascinating part of our body. It has many functions. If something affects this brain early in development, its impact will cause areas of the brain to develop differently. Depending on which areas of the brain are involved, one will find different problems. Each of these hidden disabilities, as it relates to Veronica, is described in more detail in this chapter.

VERONICA'S HIDDEN DISABILITIES

This road map helps us understand Veronica's life. (Or, if you are an adult who recognizes him- or herself in this book, it might help you to understand yourself.) It is not unusual for children, adolescents, or adults to have one or more of these disorders. The more of these hidden disorders one has, the more likely that others exist or will manifest themselves in time. So, it is not uncommon to find a child with comorbid learning disabilities and ADHD. This same child might have a tic disorder or obsessive-compulsive disorder; he or she might also be overly anxious, have trouble regulating anger, or exhibit any number of other disabilities over time.

Veronica has each of the cortical problems described. She has a language disability, a learning disability and sensory integration dysfunction. In addition, she has a mood disorder and ADHD. Over the course of her life, she has frequently struggled to control her anxiety and depression. It is unclear whether her anxiety and depression were situational—that is, related to the stresses in her life at the time they occurred—or if they were more chronic and pervasive in nature, reflecting an inherited, "modulating" disorder.

The two disorders with the greatest impact on Veronica were the learning disabilities and ADHD. Thus, I will explain these in greater detail.

Learning Disabilities

It is easiest to look at learning as an information-processing task involving one or more areas in the brain. Learning disabilities are a result of difficulties involving specific parts of this process. The first task in processing information is to receive the information and record it in the brain (i.e., *input*). Once recorded, this information must be handled in such a way that it can be understood (i.e., *integration*). The third process is storage and retrieval (i.e., *memory*). Finally, information must be communicated from the brain (i.e., *output*). Learning disabilities are defined based on this input-integration-memory-output model. Each area will be described briefly.

Input Disabilities

This central brain process is called *perception;* a person might have a visual perception disability or an auditory perception disability. Visual perception disabilities might be reflected in distinguishing subtle differences in shapes (e.g., mistaking a *d* for a *b*, or a *p* for a *q*, or a *6* and a *9*). One might have difficulty with figure-ground tasks, that is, not being able to focus on the relevant stimulus in a field of vision. Judging distance or depth is another visual-perceptual task, which causes an individual to bump into things, knock things over, or fall off a chair.

Auditory perception disabilities cause individuals to experience difficulties in the area of distinguishing subtle differences in sounds, so that they misunderstand what is being said. Many words sound similar, such as *hair* and *air*, *ball* and *bell*. Some individuals have difficulty with auditory figure-ground, so they confuse what sound to listen to when there is more than one source. An individual might not be able to process sound input quickly. He or she appears to have to think about what is heard longer than normal before understanding what is said. This is called an *auditory processing problem* or an *auditory lag*, which causes a person to appear to be lost, confused, or preoccupied when too much is said.

Integration Disabilities

When the brain records new information, at least three steps are involved. The incoming stimuli must be 1) placed in the correct order (i.e., *sequencing*), 2) understood in the context used (i.e., *abstraction*), and 3) integrated with all other incoming stimuli plus all relevant memory tracks into a concept (i.e., *organization*). One can have an integrative disability in any of these areas: sequencing, abstraction, or organization. Such a disability might affect visual or auditory inputs. Thus, a person can have visual-sequencing or auditory-sequencing disabilities, visual-abstraction or auditory-abstraction disabilities, and so forth.

Sequencing Disabilities

Sequencing disabilities can result in confusing inputs; for example, a person may write *21* for *12* or *dog* for *god*, or he or she may mix up the parts of words and mispronounce words. A child might try to explain something but start in the middle of the explanation, then go to the beginning, and finally to the end. These individuals often have difficulty using sequences. They can memorize the months of the year, for example, but are unable to say what comes after any month without starting with January and working their way up. Using the dictionary is difficult if a person cannot use the sequence of the alphabet automatically from one various starting point in the alphabet but instead has to go back to *A* each time.

Abstraction Disabilities

The inability to derive the correct meaning of a word based on how it is used can result in an abstraction disability. These individuals may have difficulty generalizing out from specific words or concepts. They might miss the meaning of jokes, puns, idioms, or other plays on words. They may appear to be paranoid because they interpret what others say in a more concrete or literal way than what is intended.

Organizational Disabilities

Organizational disabilities can result in a person having difficulty pulling multiple parts of information into a full or complete concept or in difficulty breaking down whole concepts into their parts. Such individuals may show this disorganization in other aspects of their life. Their notebooks or desks or rooms may be totally disorganized. Organizing time or making plans might be difficult. They lose things, forget things, or do their homework but forget to turn it in.

Memory Disabilities

Children or adolescents with learning disabilities usually have excellent long-term memory. They can retain information once stored. They might have difficulty, however, in *short-term memory,* the ability to concentrate on information and store it. They might learn information well while attending to it (e.g., for a spelling list), yet they will not retain this information a short time later. These students need to have many more repetitions than the average person does in order to process information into long-term memory. They can learn, but they must work on the process over time. One might have a visual short-term memory disability or an auditory short-term memory disability.

Output Disabilities

A person with output disabilities may have difficulty communicating information orally (i.e., a language disability) or in using his or her muscles (i.e., a motor coordination disorder). The individual may have a disability in one or both of these areas.

Most individuals have little difficulty with spontaneous language. They are able to initiate conversations because they have the ability and opportunity to organize thoughts and to find words before speaking. Some individuals might have difficulty when commanded to speak. If such people are asked to produce language, they must organize their thoughts and find the right words as they speak. They might speak with ease when they initiate the conversation; however, they might not be able to respond when asked a question or requested to speak. In this situation, they might struggle for words, ramble, or say the wrong word and appear to be disorganized. They might begin to speak, then forget what they were saying.

Motor Coordination Disabilities

Some people with learning disabilities will have trouble coordinating the use of groups of large muscles (i.e., gross motor disabilities). Others may have difficulty coordinating groups of small muscles (i.e., fine motor disabilities). Gross motor disabilities will result in the individual's being clumsy or having difficulty with such activities as running, climbing, or swimming. The most frequently found fine motor disability relates to writing. This skill requires the coordination of teams of small muscles. These individuals have difficulty getting their dominant hand to write in a fast and legible way. In addition to having poor handwriting, they may have difficulty with such written language tasks as spelling, grammar, spacing, capitalization, or punctuation.

THE LEARNING DISABILITY PROFILE

Each individual with a learning disability will have his or her own profile of learning abilities and learning disabilities. Each will have one or more of the disabilities described previously. There is no stereotyped individual; each must be assessed and understood individually. These learning disabilities can result in academic skill, language, or motor skill disorders.

Veronica describes having problems with visual perception, sequencing, organization, short-term memory, and written language. Her strengths are in auditory perception, auditory memory, and oral language. Veronica's combination of disabilities results in her having reading comprehension, organization, and written language problems.

Before leaving this discussion on learning disabilities, it would be helpful to look at a disorder often associated with learning disabilities, sensory integration dysfunction. This disorder has a great impact on Veronica's life.

Sensory Integration Dysfunction

This disorder relates to how the brain processes information that is needed to tell the body what to do. For example, when a person is going to tie a shoe or write or skip, how does the body know what to do in exactly the proper motor sequence? Depending on which sensory systems are involved in the sensory integration dysfunction, an individual might have problems with tactile sensitivity, body movement coordination, and/or adapting to position of body in space. Visual perception is essential and is

225

usually seen in the context of a learning disability. But there are three other sensory inputs needed for this task. When an individual has problems with one or more of these three inputs, it is called a sensory integration dysfunction.

These sensory inputs involve nerve endings in the skin (i.e., *tactile* input); nerve endings in the muscles, ligaments, and joints (i.e., *proprioception* input); and nerve endings in the inner ear (i.e., *vestibular* input). The behaviors associated with sensory integration dysfunction might reflect the incorrect perception of these inputs or might reflect the body's efforts to cope with these problems by overstimulating these inputs. Difficulties with each of these inputs are described in more detail below.

Tactile Dysfunction

Individuals with tactile difficulties confuse input from the nerve endings near the skin surface that interpret light touch. They may be tactilely defensive. From early childhood, an individual experiencing tactile perception difficulties will not like being touched or held. This child or adolescent is sensitive to touch and may perceive it as uncomfortable. He or she might complain of the roughness of clothes, irritation caused by the tag on the back of a shirt, a belt being too tight, or shoes rubbing against the socks. Often, washing or brushing hair is felt as painful, resulting in a person crying or resisting it being done. Others might not like showers or having water splashed on them at a pool. They often feel defensive and need a larger space around their body. They do not like sitting in circles or being close to others. Someone lightly brushes against him or her and the child gets angry. These problems usually lessen by about age 7 but can continue into adolescence or adulthood.

Some children with this problem can handle being touched or held if they can prepare and be in control. They might initiate the hug. Parents must learn to announce when they plan to hug and to do so from the front so the child can see what is happening. An unexpected touch or hug will not be appreciated.

226

Some feel so deprived of touch that they try to compensate by doing controlled touching. These are the children who walk around the classroom touching other children, often perceived by others as annoying. They anger classmates and teachers.

Proprioception Perception

Problems with proprioception perception relate to motor planning activities. The proprioceptors inform the brain which muscle parts are contracted or relaxed and which joints are bent or extended. This information is needed for the brain to know what each part of the body is doing so that the next step in a motor sequence can be initiated. Individuals with problems in this area might have difficulty with gross motor planning activities (i.e., using groups of large muscles to do a task) or with fine motor planning activities (i.e., using groups of small muscles to do a task).

As discussed previously, gross motor activities include walking, running, jumping, and skipping. Fine motor activities include buttoning, zipping, tying, using eating utensils, and writing. Individuals with gross motor problems may be clumsy. They hold their pencils with an awkward grasp and write poorly. They often do not do well in sports that require quick eye–hand coordination. Some children compensate for this deprivation by overstimulating their muscles and joints. They jump, bump into things, flap their hands, or hop.

Vestibular Perception

The vestibular perception function refers to the task of knowing where your body is in space; that is, where it is in relation to gravity. Vestibular inputs are needed to interact with space and to sense body movements in space, such as adjusting to changes in position. This child might avoid climbing or sudden changes in position. Adolescents and adults might not like elevators or escalators. Sudden changes in position or lack of certainty as to where one is in space can cause anxiety. Visual input assists in these tasks. Thus, when this input is limited (eyes closed; being in an area where the walls, floor, ceiling are similar in color) it causes confusion and anxiety. Vestibular input helps the brain keep those muscles involved with opposing gravity toned and ready to be used. Many individuals with vestibular problems have weak upper trunk muscles because of the lack of stimulation. Some individuals compensate for this deficit by overstimulating the vestibular system. They might rock, head bang, spin, or swing.

ATTENTION-DEFICIT/HYPERACTIVITY DISORDER

Three types of behaviors are associated with ADHD: hyperactivity, inattentiveness, or impulsiveness. One might exhibit one, two, or all three of these behaviors. These behaviors are congenital, that is, present since earliest childhood. They are also pervasive, occurring during every aspect of life, throughout the day.

Hyperactivity

Very young children exhibiting hyperactivity might run around the room and be very active. Most children are fidgety or squirmy. By adolescence, the behaviors may be less obvious, with the individual conducting fidgety activities with fingers or exhibiting restlessness. Many adults try to channel this behavior into their work; however, when resting their fingers or legs begin to move.

Distractibility

Some individuals have difficulty filtering out unimportant stimuli in their environment. They are easily distracted and have short attention spans. Some people are distracted by sounds, others by visual images.

Adolescents and adults often complain of internal distractibility. Their own thoughts distract them. They might try to concentrate but their minds wander or they daydream a lot. Or, they might have several thoughts at the same time and jump from one thought or activity to another.

Impulsivity

Usually, we stop and think before we talk or act. Some people with ADHD are not able to do this. They speak before they think, interrupting or calling out. They might say something and hurt someone's feelings because they did not think before speaking. They might act before thinking, resulting in risk-taking behaviors or poor judgment.

The ADHD Profile

It is important to understand that some people are hyperactive, some are inattentive, some are impulsive, and some have a mixture of two of these behaviors. It appears that these behaviors decrease or fade away by puberty in about 30%–40% of children. For the remainder, however, the problems continue into adulthood.

THE MODULATION DISORDERS

I described in the section for understanding neurologically based disorders the set of tasks the brain has to do in order to maintain emotional equilibrium. If any of these essential functions are not operating effectively, individuals may have problems related to modulating specific moods or behaviors. It is important to distinguish between anxiety, depression, or anger-control difficulties that are related to specific life stresses and similar problems that are a result of faulty wiring in this area of the brain. With situational problems, the difficulties usually begin at a certain time or are related to certain life experiences. The neurologically caused problems are present from birth and manifest themselves as a chronic and pervasive pattern of difficulties. Veronica has had many life crises. Her level of anxiety, panic experiences, and depression have been present since early childhood, and they occur in every aspect of her life. Starting probably in early adolescence, if not earlier, she began to experience mood swings.

As an older adult she was finally diagnosed with bipolar disorder (formerly called *manic-depressive disorder*). She was no longer experiencing periods of depression and periods of normal moods. She began to experience what are called *hypomanic episodes,* in which individuals find that their minds are racing and their bodies are overactive. They cannot relax or turn off their thoughts. They might talk excessively, be very active and productive, and stay on a "high" for days. During this time, they might not eat or sleep. I suspect that Veronica did not experience these hypomanic episodes as clearly when she was an adolescent because of the alcohol and drugs she was using. It is not an uncommon history to find that people with bipolar disorder also have a history of alcohol and/or drug use.

This depression-to-euphoria mood swing is often associated with another type of mood swing, when one changes from being pleasant to being in a rage. Some people can be calm and amiable and then rapidly swing into periods of anger and rage. Veronica's demonstrated patterns of both types of mood swings led to her diagnosis of bipolar disorder.

CONCLUSION

Veronica struggles with so many hidden disabilities. Her book describes her struggles with each. Her life describes the price one pays when these disabilities are not recognized, diagnosed, and addressed.

Her purpose in writing this book is to sensitize her readers to these disabilities, provide insights on how they might be recognized, and describe what happens if they are not recognized. She exposes her pain and some very personal stories about her life in the hope that others will experience a better life because they saw themselves or someone they knew in it, and changed their lives for the better.

I join her in believing that early recognition and early intervention are the best strategies for treating these disabilities and are the best prevention for future emotional and social problems. I, too, hope that readers will be more sensitive and more informed.

INDEX